On Bumping Into God

Kenneth
F. Hall

D1258993

WARNER PRESS
ANDERSON INDIANA

Printed in the United States of America

Contents

A Word about the Title

Right off the bat I have revealed some things about myself through the use of this title. In fairness to you I need to explain some of the biases I bring into this book. Maybe I can do it by explaining the title: *On Bumping into God*.

You see, I bumped into a man the other day. No, I didn't literally collide with him, awkward and inattentive as I sometimes am. It happened down at Meridian and Tenth and was entirely unplanned, at least on my part. I was looking for a pair of shoes and didn't have this man in mind at all. He wasn't lost or in hiding somewhere and if I had wanted to see him, I could have gone to his house or called him on the phone. It was all kind of accidental, happened because he's around town a lot and I was down there at the time. Our talk was brief and routine even though it turned out we had some important things to say to each other. He didn't force himself on me or grab my arm and hold me there. It was just a casual meeting.

Now I don't really want to push this as an analogy. I'm simply saying that it is my viewpoint—one that you might as well know right now runs all through this book—that man does meet God. Sometimes this may be a dramatic encounter. Sometimes it is a casual, even accidental meeting. Sometimes it happens as a result of some planning. Sometimes it fully engages man with God. But I have the feeling that when most modern men meet God, they haven't been out seeking for a lost God somewhere. After all, it is not God who is lost. They're not on a safari. They may not even believe that a God exists, at least in any way that is important in their lives. And so what happens for them is a "bumping into." I figure most of the time that's true for me, even though out of faith, love, and hope, I do see God as the one I have met.

When modern man does meet God, it is often the kind of casual encounter that may leave him wondering just what happened and who it was and how it was.

You see more biases coming out now. I am proceeding here on an assumption that we all run into what the man of hope and faith calls God. Only, the man who isn't operating by any traditional Christian faith or hope may use other terms. These terms may depend on his background, experience, and vocabulary. He may suddenly recognize one day that he has been wondering about himself and his life and the meaning of it all. And then somewhere he finds a sense of basic meaning. I figure he's been bumping into God.

Somebody else concludes that outside himself and his friends and the world around him there is something Other. Bumping into God. Somebody else, with a philosophical turn of mind, looks all around him and concludes there must be an Ultimate Reality. Another of quite different mentality sees indications of the Supernatural. Another sees in things a purpose and order that seem to be apart from all that he can understand in nature or lay hands on. Bumping into God. Of course, a more abiding relationship exists, but we're concerned with starting points and foundation stones.

This book will look at some ways man becomes engaged with God. These relationships will be examined for what they may show us about how God relates himself to us. Our concern will be more on this relationship than on any rigid catalogue of the characteristics of God or of man. We shall be trying to see God in the ways he deals with man.

We'll be looking at some of the common misunderstandings about God's role as men react after their meetings with him. We'll be looking for new insights into how God relates to his world that can grow out of the times when we bump into God.

This kind of title suggests, perhaps too strongly, that God is real primarily as he comes into contact with the daily life of people right here and now. That certainly seems to be how he can be known best. This is God, here and now, or immanent in history and in our personal lives. But I don't claim to be capturing very much of God with this approach—only a small part of a vast affirmation about him.

I write as a Christian, as a follower of Jesus of Nazareth. That means that among my biases here is the idea that God is revealed supremely in Jesus Christ. No other life can so reveal him, no events, no writing about him begins to compare with the way I come to know God through Jesus Christ himself.

I also believe that God is so immeasurably beyond our grasp that we can't really claim to sum him up in terms of our relationship with him here and now. He also operates in the broad universe far out beyond our capacities to meet him, going beyond every human sense. But for the most part I take that on faith and don't look at it as a thing to be argued about or proved on any other grounds than personal expectations, experience, and the Bible itself—all of which we take with faith and hope.

TO GROUPS STUDYING THIS BOOK TOGETHER

You will notice at the end of each chapter a section called Thinking Things Through. This is designed to help you use some group process together as you explore this book. The section provides possibilities for goal setting for study sessions related to the chapter, some basic discussion questions, and some possible learning activities. From this material the teacher may readily develop a teaching plan for a session or work with a committee to do this.

Ten sessions. Note that there are ten chapters and therefore ready guidance for ten sessions which could be held once a week or on a more concentrated basis.

Thirteen sessions. Occasionally a class in the church school might want to consider the book for thirteen weeks or a full quarter. Here the ten chapters might readily expand to thirteen as you linger with any chapter that seems to demand more attention by the class. For more specific suggestions, however, we suggest the following: Divide chapter 3 into three areas, considering in consecutive sessions God as Father, God as he comes to us in Christ, and God as expressed in the Holy Spirit. Divide chapter 7 into two areas, spending one session on God in history in general and another on God's work through the church. Or, other ways of dividing may suit your own situation better.

Five Sessions. For a briefer but more concentrated study the book may be approached by studying two chapters in connection with each session. Possible combinations: Chapters 1 and 3, looking at God as Father, as revealed in Christ, as revealed through the Holy Spirit, and in nature. Chapters 2 and 5, considering God as close to us and involved with us in the world and as the great transcendant Lord. Chapters 4 and 7, God revealed through the Bible, through history, and in the life of the church. Chapters 6 and 8, some of the problems and opportunities related to knowing God—faith and doubt, evil, suffering, and death. Chapters 9 and 10, coming to God in prayer, commitment, and affirmation.

1

"Fine Day, Isn't It?"

You bump into somebody and the first thing you know, you start talking about the weather. Maybe it's about the only thing you know you have in common. It is something you can talk about pleasantly without getting into politics or religion or something very personal. In this day of environmental crisis, however, maybe even the weather is no longer a safe, casual subject.

Now, suppose this somebody you are bumping into is God? Do you talk with him about the weather? Just how casual do you get? And just what has the weather got to do with God, anyhow?

IT'S THE LORD'S WEATHER—OR IS IT?

The custodian at Old Main where I went to college was a cheerful, optimistic, and devout man. Rain or shine, snow or sleet, he always gave us a grin when we walked into the building and tracked over his floors. "It's the Lord's weather, brother," he'd say. As several generations of young men and women went through that school, whether or not they learned Greek or geometry or Physical Education 112, they did come out knowing that whatever the elements did, it was the Lord's weather.

More recently, however, we hear about experiments at seeding clouds in order to produce rain over drought-stricken areas. We know about efforts at controlling tropical storms. We have learned how air pollution can increase the incidence of thunderstorms, raise or lower temperatures, perhaps change whole climates. And so here, too, man has begun to take a hand in the Lord's weather.

Still, men of faith have seen the weather and, in fact, all of the universe as the creative work of God and a means of understanding something more about him. Others have been content to see the universe as simply the product of natural forces. Some of them have stood scoffing that the God they heard described by Christians as kind and loving could be understood through a creation in which occur disastrous earthquakes, killer tornadoes, and destructive floods.

The man of faith has looked at the universe and in it has seen God at work (Psalms 102:25; 104:5). He has pointed to its beauty. The young green overlay on a spring meadow, the liquid silver of a tiny waterfall, the flashing crimson of a cardinal in the snow, the fragrance and warm loveliness of a rose—these have spoken of a Creator with an eye to beauty, an appreciation of the lovely. After all, they have said, the world could have been created in plain old black and white and without symmetry, contrast, and rhythm. The man of faith says, surely, this reflects something about a Creator God.

The man of faith has pointed to the orderliness and dependability of the universe. The exact minute when the sun will rise and set is known for years to come. The sun, moon, and stars move on their orderly courses. The seasons come and go and climates stay within the narrow range of tolerances that permit life. Even such unusual events as eclipses and comet showers can be predicted with precision. Is such regularity and precision a product of cosmic coincidence? Could all the parts of a watch be placed in a box and shaken until eventually they would all come together into a machine that begins to mark the time?

10

If the orderliness could be explained as a product of one chance in an infinite number of chances, still the man of faith would say that behind it was God. If the orderliness were explained as a product of natural forces blended together systematically and fully understood in scientific terms, the man of faith would still say that the author of it all is God.

The man of faith has looked at the majesty and vastness of the world and seen it as reflecting the greatness and power of the God who made it. More far ranging than the trillions of miles between stars must be this God. Stronger than the explosions on the surface of the sun must he be. More majestic than the towering Grand Tetons, more deep than the deeps of the rolling seas.

The man of faith has looked at creation and in it found what appears to him to be intelligent provision for life, for creative development. The operating laws of the universe make sense, and they seem to reflect more than casual thoughtfulness. There is the balance to be found in nature. One species finds its food among another and helps to keep that species in proper proportion. Plant and animal life moves through cycles that have their own meanings and beauty and progression. The air we breathe moves and is freshened. Natural agents are present in the world to battle infection and disease. Gravity enables us to walk and move about in our environment. What seems to us to be great laws of the universe operate for the good of plant and animal and man.

Others have looked beyond the orderliness and beauty of the universe and claim to recognize God in the unusual and mysterious which they cannot explain through natural law. If the sun appeared to stand still, then that must be God. If a disease is healed suddenly or without medical explanation, then that is ascribed to God. If a dry path of escape is carved out of a rolling sea, then that is God's work. Some observers see in this attitude a "God of the gaps." Whatever couldn't be explained by natural law and science, then that must be God.

While we might be perfectly content for God to be understood as a God of miracles or a God of the mysterious, there is a danger here. If God is seen *primarily* as working through what is at present unexplained by science, we are placing him in those gaps in our knowledge which are constantly being reduced as science and other disciplines explain more and more. God needs to be seen both in the known and the unknown, his work understood in terms of both, in harmony with all the universe, if our comprehension of him and his ways is going to be soundly based.

The person who doesn't see God at work in creation usually points to a number of problems. Christians experience a personal God, but there is a great deal of apparent impersonalness in the natural world God authors. It rains on the just and the unjust. In fact nature may at times seem to victimize innocent and righteous persons. Just as there is beauty (by our normal standards) in nature, there is also ugliness. While there are signs of provision, wisdom, and sustaining qualities, there are also signs of disorder and lack of continuity. Even as signs of loving care show up, so do other observers find what they call vengeance and lack of concern. There is a kind of injustice seen in the operation of the universe, and sometimes it seems that for every worthy quality in the world there are qualities opposed to the good life of man.

Where does this leave us? With a draw between those who choose to use the natural order as an argument for God and those who choose to say it proves nothing? You probably have already made up your own mind. The man of faith tends to use the beauty, orderliness, sustaining quality, and wisdom he finds in the natural order to undergird his faith. That is where I stand. I gather strength from

Jesus' reminder that just as God is concerned with the lilies of the field and all the rest of his creation, so he is concerned for me. "But if God so clothes the grass of the field, which today is alive and tomorrow is thrown into the oven, will he not much more clothe you, O men of little faith?" (Matthew 6:30). But all this still leaves us without a sure-fire argument from creation that wins *everyone* to faith in God. To argue from creation to the existence of an intelligent Creator has its strengths and comforts, but it is not a complete answer.

Knowing the Creator personally, then, we can understand some things about the creation and in turn learn from them. Assuming there is a God behind creation, his work would seem to say to us that he does not play favorites. Everybody gets treated just about the same by the forces of nature—it rains on the just and the unjust alike. We get a picture of a God behind this creation who does operate in an orderly and systematic fashion, with a universe full of vast detail and great majesty. But God is affirmed first by faith and not through observation of his work.

The more science uncovers about the workings of the world, the more conscious we become of how all the parts of creation are interrelated. Few things operate with complete independence in the world, without affecting or being affected by other elements. All the recent stress on the ecology of our environment has demonstrated this very interrelatedness. All creation sits on a delicate balance. One part of it depends on another. One part puts out a chemical product needed by another. The narrow range of temperature, air make-up, moisture required for life, hangs in a delicate balance within this vast creation. Man has developed the capacity to upset such a balance. If there is a message from God to us here, it is: You are created interdependent with each other and with all parts of this vast creation. You have a mission to maintain the balance and to sense your oneness with all that has been made. This is what having dominion over God's world (Genesis 1:26, Psalm 8) and being a good steward in God's world indicate.

So man meets God in the constant setting of God's creation. God speaks to man about himself through what he has created and through the ongoing, life-renewing, creative process in which he lives and moves. God speaks to man as day after day he sustains this world he has made. God and man meet as they share in the creative work of the world for which God has especially designed man. The man of faith ascribes that creative spark he finds in himself, that bit of talent, that muscle for work, to the creator God who made and sustains him.

OUR DAILY GOD

So God has something to do with the weather. So he has created us and helps us keep going. So, somehow, he is tied in closely with the ever-developing history through which we live. The relationship can be close, and for some people it can be casual. This day-by-day, hour-by-hour contact with God can take on various forms, many of which can enrich our lives, ennoble our way of living, inspire us to achievement beyond ourselves. At the same time, like every other good thing, people can start taking God for granted. They can become too casual about this God who is truly so very near us but who is also the great, exalted Lord of the universe. Look now at some of these ideas about our relationship with this God and consider how they best reflect who God is and what he means in our lives.

"God and I are co-workers." It's a good feeling to be on God's team, to sense the human dignity, and importance, and worth that is in man. We have been given high

abilities, as well as a high responsibility. It appears that, somehow, in working in his world, God relies on the people he has created to work with him. Often, where man does not do the work God has left to him, it simply doesn't get done. Certainly, Paul felt himself to be a co-worker with God and he infused this spirit in those around him (2 Cor. 6:1).

A couple of old stories reflect what seems to happen here. One day the minister walked past the garden where old Jake was painfully hoeing his peas and tomatoes. The plot was neatly cultivated, the plants were growing vigorously, and an abundant harvest was on its way. "My, God and you are doing a wonderful job on this garden," beamed the minister. Jake rubbed his aching back and looked the minister straight in the eye. "You shoulda seen this garden when the Lord had it all to himself."

The relationship of a partnership, however, can have all kinds of proportions. For instance, there was the recipe for elephant-rabbit stew: One rabbit and one elephant. How much rabbit are you going to taste? So it goes with any kind of partnership man feels he has with God. Sometimes we take God's part of the relationship for granted. We may actually set ourselves up as the senior partner and make God the errand boy when in fact it is the other way around. Away with arrogance when we proclaim ourselves as workers together with God! In with humility and a sense of proper proportion. When something is accomplished, it is God working in and through us. In that sense we are junior partners with God.

"God is my friend." The song puts it: "What a friend we have in Jesus." Unique in all the religious world is the concept we find in Christianity that the great God we worship can also be our friend. He loves us. He is concerned about us. We share in all of life together. Surely God does come to us in such a close and intimate fellowship. He

15

came to Moses, we are told in Exodus 33:11, as friend to friend, and God's relationship to Moses was not at this point unique.

As with any friendship, we can abuse the privileges. We can begin to take things too much for granted. We may lose our sense of glory and awe in the relationship. In the whole process we may forget that God is also the great and holy one, the high-and-lifted-up King of Glory. We may forget the responsibilities of friendship, which is after all a two-way street. God helps us, brings love and fellowship to us. Our call is to return it to him and to express that same kind of feeling to those around us. Because God is a friend to us, we become a friend to others, including those who have special need, those to whom we might not normally feel attracted.

So the God who daily is so with us comes as the most noble and highest kind of friend, not a weak, palsy-walsy sentimentalist. How much his noble friendship can mean in our lives.

"In the Name of God." Devout Christians, many of them in a generation now disappearing, have been concerned to express the daily events in their lives in terms of their constant relationship to God. They lace their speech with such phrases as "The Lord willing." For some, this may be only habitual and for others it may express a kind of routine reliance on God they don't really feel. The balance of relationship comes here in expressing and giving public witness to one's relationship with God, in acknowledging him as Lord of our lives and doing this without expressing a false overdependency or in making a mere display of our religion. Checkpoints: Is this habit only? Do I really feel that I want this to be within the will of God? Is this humility being voiced or is it pride?

"God speaks." God does speak. Looking back from our vantagepoint, we know now that God spoke through the

prophet Amos when he said, "Thus says the Lord." But not everybody recognized it at the time. Maybe it comes clear that God speaks through a daring and insightful minister with a clear word of Good News to share. A devout and sensitive saint of God may have something significant to say.

At the same time, a nagging question persists. Not given the test of time and the long proof or experience that affirms the Bible, how do we really know if God is speaking in current situations? Maybe a person has so closely identified himself and his own wishes with some falsely projected image of God that everything he personally wants he thinks God also wants. Maybe he so much wants to marry the Widow Jones that he tells her this is God's will. And maybe the good widow finds it necessary to reply, "If it is, God hasn't yet told me." So it is that some persons fall into the trap of casually identifying their own private wishes with the will of God. Such persons need the concern and help of the Christian community to know the difference between their own desires and the will of God—no easy matter.

God does speak through people as they act in history. It calls for a sensitive ear to hear and then the courage to speak out. Perception, courage, and grace are all involved. The too-casual approach to all of this can be harmful. And when the word is spoken, Christian dialogue about its place and significance is in order since no one human voice can claim to speak for God without challenge and discerning discussion. And without the support of the Christian community and the test of time.

"The Inner Light." This term speaks of something of a mystical relationship with God. Of course, mystics and mysticism come in all shapes and sizes. Certainly, there are those who live in such apparent harmony with the purposes of God that we can understand how God does

enter into their lives. He illumines the way of life for them. We have been so made that God can dwell within us, guiding and inspiring and empowering us. He may light up truth for us, through our insights, our consciences, and our common sense. He does, however, remain an Other, distinct enough from us that we can get to know him and experience him. He is God and we are separate persons. Let there be no confusion: no matter how close a person lives to God, he does not himself become God.

"God is in his world." God is not lost, nor is he so hidden that he cannot be identified. God is in his world but is not so merged with it that he and it are the same thing. Thus a poet who has become something of a pantheist thinks he sees the actual God in the blooming of a rose. Thus a philosopher may find meaning in the world as he sees it rooted in God who is in it and through it all. But if all is God, what special meaning is there left to him? The man of faith finds something special in God, something that makes a difference, something that stirs in him a sense of awe and worship, something Other to whom he can give his loyalty and dedication. It would seem to be a terribly casual feeling to experience God everywhere around outside and inside, the essense of everything that is.

God is here. He lives and works and moves through his world and the people in it.

What are we saying? That God is only far away and high and lifted up? That God is best known only as the majestic and powerful force that created the world? That we have to keep some distance between ourselves and him? Not really. God cannot be bottled up in some kind of prescription that limits him in either direction. He is both high and lifted up and near at hand. But he is Other. Whatever we will isn't automatically his will. He is personal and we are personal and at those meeting places between us, there is man potentially at his best and God potentially at his greatest. There is where life and love are most real.

THINKING THINGS THROUGH

Some Goals

To explore how God relates himself to us through his creative work in the world.

To understand that God does relate himself to us, both as the great Creator of the world and the day-by-day Sustainer of our lives.

To consider what makes up an appropriate relationship for man with God on a day-by-day basis that can be either too-distant or too-casual.

Some Questions to Consider

1. If the natural creation of the world is supposed to show us something about the Creator, what do the deserts, the trackless arctic fields, the natural catastrophes, say?

2. What limits to understanding God would you place on the natural order of our world? What other means of God's revelation would you rank higher?

3. What does the interdependence of man and the rest of creation—as increasingly demonstrated by ecology—say about man and his place and responsibility in the created world?

4. Do you agree that man can take a too-casual attitude toward God? What are reasons for and against this?

5. How would you describe your own relationship with God—casual? distant? varying from day to day? respectfully close?

Some Things to Do

1. Collect a variety of nature scenes from magazines and work with other persons to identify what these may be saying about the creator God. What was man's part, if any, in the scene? Have you collected some scenes that don't show only the beauty of the earth, by our standards?

2. Look at a series of pictures of people, considering them also as part of God's creation. In what sense have they been created by God? by themselves? by their families? by the society in which they live?

3. Go on a nature walk, pausing to discuss God's creative work with others or writing down your own reactions as you go. Consider the possibilities of a nature walk within the city, if that is where you live.

4. Get in a small group and pretend that half of you have a very, very casual relationship with God. How would you talk about God in such a situation? What help might be shared among the group?

2

"What's a Nice God Like You Doing in a Place Like This?"

I never expected to meet you here, God. The trash hasn't been collected along this street for weeks. The place stinks. Here is a sleezy bar. Across the alley are the dirty windows of a poolroom. Over there is a flophouse. The sunlight shines in here for only an hour at high noon.

I didn't really think you'd be here, God. This huge room is so crowded, so busy. This is the world's money marketplace. Traders rush here and there, executing orders. Specialists frantically seek to keep their stocks running on an even keel. The big board flashes its messages of stocks sold, prices rising, prices falling, fortunes lost and made. Strain lines the faces of these men. I thought money was god here, and I didn't look for You.

I didn't think you'd be here, God, surely not here. For this is the place of the enemy. The people in this country are a threat to our way of life. They hold an alien political philosophy. One of their leaders said they would bury us. These people stir up trouble against us wherever they can around the world, and they send enemy agents to undermine our lives at home. No, I didn't expect to find you here.

A "NICE" GOD?

God often surprises us about where he turns up because in our encounters with him we may have come to a too-

21

narrow understanding of who he is and how he works. Deliberately or accidentally some of us have come to see our God as a nice little old gentleman. Without realizing it we may somehow picture him as a sleek and suave man wearing white gloves who feels along the tops of the door frames for dust and wipes off a chair before sitting in it. We can readily see him in a polished church pew on a Sunday morning, with sunlight sifting through the stained-glass windows to illumine his beaming face. We may be able to see him as a gentleman farmer out walking through his fields, pausing to admire fat cattle behind white fences in a green pasture under a bright blue sky. It would be a little harder for us to see him butchering hogs or sweatily stowing hay in a barn mow. It's easy to picture him in an air-conditioned boardroom, meeting with executives around a conference table, but hard to see him wrestling a piggot of iron coming out of a blast furnace.

Perhaps what we are really dealing with here is not a "nice" God so much as a good and great and wonderfully righteous God. He is not trained or domesticated for our convenience, but out of his rugged goodness and his firm righteousness he does come to us with love and compassion. Here is the kind of God who is going to have the highest appeal to the man on the street, rather than any meek and mild, convenient image some well-meaning persons may pass along. We say quite a bit about God to this easily-turned-off-and-on man on the street in several areas which we now shall put under the spotlight.

Our Open Witness. This can clarify or confuse the average man about God. If someone makes a big display of his religion and his high devotion, he may pass along the impression that this is what his God wants: the big display. There is this fine line between witnessing to what you are under God and making a parade of it. It's the difference between the Pharisee Jesus pointed to who made much of his public prayers and the sinner who sincerely but quietly asked forgiveness. We miss the mark if we portray merely a nice God with our public witness instead of the great and righteous God.

But being fearful of giving a wrong impression dare not drive us away from the joy, privilege, and responsibility of making a public statement with our lives about the God we know. Fear of sham dare not drive us away from putting our faith in words, in service in the name of God, in action in the spirit of Christ.

The Humble Attitude. Here we are with the most astounding good news in all the world to share. Here we are with word about the great and good God. Surely there is something to be proud of, to call out from the highest mountain. And out there are all the world's great needs and the vast spread of wrong and shortcoming all around us. We have this message to share. We have this feeling that God has done great things for us, which he needs to do for others.

Down through the centuries the Christian response to this has been one of great humility. The more God has done for us the more quiet about it some people have become. Maybe they are reacting to that minority of people who develop a vast spiritual pride about their kinship with God. These are the holier-than-thou people who say, "I have the final word of truth, and this is it. You are wrong. Look how good and righteous I am and how deceived, dirty, and sinful you are." Lo, such people indeed do great harm.

But perhaps one of their most harmful results is in shutting the mouths of Christians from publicly voicing their faith and making forthright statements of what they believe to be right. Our righteous God would like for us to speak out boldly about him and his righteousness in the face of the sickness all around us in the world. Particularly is the young convert susceptible here. Out of his new faith he enthusiastically blurts out the good news that has come to him. He gets rebuffed as a result. Well-meaning fellow Christians seek to hush him up. Pretty soon he becomes a silent conformer to the conspiracy of silent Christian witness that leaves the story untold.

The Depths of Faithfulness. Sometimes God is used as mere window dressing, to add a note of decorum, to bring a kind of divine blessing to whatever is done. Such is the tendency on the part of those on the edges of Christianity to twist some surface and shallow notions about God and religious practices to meet their own purposes.

In reality those who come to more than a casual meeting with God find that something pretty deep is involved: a faithfulness, a commitment that pushed past surface things. For again we are not dealing here with a merely nice God but a God of the heights and depths, a God of total faithfulness. Let's apply the implications of all of this to some of our common religious practices, most of which can be matters of either mere window dressing or significant depth pointing to the reality of God.

1. Religious ceremonies. Invocations, benedictions at public gatherings, references to God in political speeches, the singing of religious songs at otherwise secular programs—they are some of the things that fall under our spotlight to consider what they may be communicating about God to the average pagan who looks on Christianity from the outside. It is not for us to look at these matters to judge the intent and spirit of everyone who engages in them. That is to be left to God. But when the late Peter Marshall was chaplain of the United States Senate, he regularly succeeded by the freshness and vigor of his prayers to make of them what seemed to be valid expressions of the ministry of God.

Some people would have us do away with routine invocations at public meetings as shallow, empty, and downright injurious to real Christianity. But such prayers do offer opportunity for men of faith to communicate validly with their God and for some word of genuine faith to be broadcast among those present. Every opportunity to name the name of God in reverence and with devotion looks like an opportunity to express a faithfulness of relation to the God we serve. At the same time these are challenges to name the name of God in fresh, exciting ways that stand a chance of building genuine God-awareness among those present and of drawing some to him.

2. God and the Three R's. The situation in public schools is much akin to what we have been discussing. Perhaps U.S. Supreme Court rulings against officially prescribed prayers and Bible readings can actually do the Christian cause a favor if they eliminate what was in some cases an empty custom. Small doses of empty religious custom can actually immunize persons against the real thing. At the same time it would also appear that the way is still open in schools and elsewhere in our society for religion to be discussed and brought actively to bear upon current life situations as a part of whole education for the whole person. Certainly Christians will want to do this at every legitimate opportunity. We have met God; we are engaged with him; we proceed to introduce him into every situation where we live and work.

3. "Bless This Food." Most families for whom God is important either have table graces and family worship regularly or feel guilty about not having it. Anything that is routine, is not thought through frequently, and is rather habitual, can become meaningless for at least some of the participants. For others the very regularity and steadiness of the undertaking takes on deep significance, because this says constantly that God is with us, we are related to him, and he does provide for us and sustain us.

It is helpful then if God's sustaining presence with us can be acknowledged regularly but in fresh and creative and significant ways. What will bring variety to the thanks at table? What can change the pace of family worship? A fresh bumping into God each day can be full of new interest, vitality, and surprising results.

4. Assembling Ourselves Together. We meet God at church. Of course, we don't meet God just at church. Of course, living the gospel on Monday is at least as important as singing about it in church on Sunday. Of course, practical Christian service deserves a place high on our priority list. Yet, in a unique way, we do meet God at the worship services of the church. There we meet him in company with others who have come for the same purpose. Their spirits join with ours. There we meet him on an exalted and inspiring basis, accompanied by music and the special beauty of the sanctuary, undergirded by shared prayer.

Here the Bible is read by someone other than yourself and it enters your mind through the gate of the ear. Here the message of the gospel is brought to you by a spokesman of God, perhaps one you also know personally as your pastor. And through it all we become engaged with God. We respond with the psalmist: "I was glad when they said to me, let us go to the house of the Lord!"

At the same time there no doubt are times when you find all of this less than a direct meeting place with God. Perhaps you climbed out of bed on the wrong side in the morning or there was too much rush and confusion in getting ready for church. Maybe you were in the down part of your emotional cycle. Maybe something is bothering you to the point you can't shake it off in the service. Maybe you were somehow out of tune with the emphasis of the service for the day. When this sort of thing happens you're out of synchronization with all that's happening and you know it. Then it's hard to feel that you are meeting God in the worship service.

The same feeling can come more subtly when the church service settles back into a mere routine for us, when we shrink the importance of the God we meet on Sunday morning to that time and place. Singing a hymn out of habit without weighing its words or letting our emotions be carried along can do more harm than good. Listening to a sermon without thinking, or thoughtlessly going through the motions of worship can all foster a shallow religion.

How sad it would be if we could not assemble ourselves regularly for worship! What a high privilege it is. But it is sometimes an abused privilege, with the result that here God comes but is not able to get through to us. Lives are not changed thereby. On the other hand, when we come fully alive, eager, alert, creative, we bring much to the service and receive back in full measure from it.

5. Living with Christian realism. Living in conscious relationship with God helps us to face the world with realism rather than sentimentality. It helps us put important weight on important matters and less emphasis on lighter issues.

Living the life of Christian realism involves being the same person through and through, the same as we stand before God as when we stand before our neighbor, the same every day of the week. The non-Christian looking on from the outside readily sees any hypocrisy he finds there and raises it as a barrier between him and the faith.

Attitudes both of unreasoning optimism and pessimism can get in the road of reality. Too much optimism is not the same thing as faith or Christian hope. It can be merely a sentimental, lackadaisical longing for better things that gets in the way of coming face to face realistically with God and his will.

27

In fact there is a kind of sentimental attitude toward people and life that can be a stumbling block in the way of genuine and realistic God-relatedness. This is the kind of attitude that focuses on the loveliness of a hymn but does not really hear its prodding message. This is the kind of attitude that fully appreciates the picture of a beautiful church steeple in a New England countryside on a church magazine cover, but greatly dislikes the picture of an ugly old man, wracked by illness and dope, lying on a Bowery sidewalk. The sentimentalist understands God only in the beautiful picture. The realist understands both as speaking to us about God. The pessimist, I suppose, would wonder about God having anything·to do with either scene.

The realistic look, one that is open eyed to things as they are and faces up to them, seeks to apply the proper priorities. When we don't take such an open-eyed view, we can get lost in our imagination, in our dreams, in our prejudices, and in the accidental distortions that develop. Without this view we can get bogged down in everything from the classic question: How many angels can dance on the head of a pin? to, Is it all right to go on Sunday afternoon picnics? And in the process, God is called to the side of people who are using false priorities and is "used" to speak for them against all balance and reality.

And so it is that we come in contact with and seek to live in the spirit of a God who is not just nice, but great and righteous altogether.

"IN A PLACE LIKE THIS"

If we understand God to be merely "nice," it may be hard to picture him even having anything to do with a crude, often dirty, sometimes evil, world like the one we live in. With that kind of image in mind, it is easy to conclude that to draw close to God the best way is to try to escape from the distractions and wrongs of this world. For that reason the founders of one midwest college established it in the middle of the last century deep in a rural area and advertised to prospective students that it was twenty miles from the nearest known form of sin.

For similar reasons we sometimes seek to draw nearer to God by going on "retreats." Usually, a retreat is held in one of nature's beauty spots, far from urban distractions. It is off the beaten path.

The same way of thinking, carried perhaps to its more ultimate extreme, characterized the whole monastic movement. Isolated monasteries, convents, and abbeys were built to house ascetic movements. Brothers and sisters would commit themselves to lives of poverty and austerity. Some would take vows of silence, never speaking to another person, and especially to a person outside the order. Some would never leave the isolated compound for the rest of their lives.

This is not to say that such urges in man to retreat from the distractions and evils of the world are mistaken. It is to say that if we can understand God *only* as withdrawn from the hurly-burly world, cut off from its evils, then we may have a distorted picture of him.

Sometimes Christians may not be able to withdraw into a monastic community, but they still seek to separate themselves from the world in order to feel a nearness to God. They do this in varied ways. Some earn their livings in shops or stores and rub shoulders every hour with "people of the world," but they put up an invisible—well, almost—curtain around them to keep themselves from being defiled. They make it perfectly clear to those around them that they and their God are a breed apart. Only when they go into the house of worship or when they gather with other Christians can they relax, because they feel themselves to be only strangers and pilgrims in this unfriendly world, and they feel separated from God when they are out in it.

This suspicion and hostility toward the world often finds itself expressed in a spirit of otherworldliness that seeks to avoid or modify all the customs of society. It may mean that the person seeks less after material things—and that can be very helpful. It may mean that the person takes on certain habits and practices that mark him as belonging to a peculiar religious culture. Thus we have the Old Order Amish with their horses and buggies and their plain garb. No doubt God honors some of this effort at being a "peculiar," set-apart people, so long as it doesn't isolate people so much that personal salvation cannot be communicated or concern for social problems out there in the world cannot be effectively expressed.

Jesus himself offered us some kind of example here. He did not get so swallowed up in his world that you couldn't tell him from the rest of the people. He had a message which he proclaimed boldly, and it set him and his people apart from the crowd. He knew how to withdraw from the clamor of the crowd for times when he could be alone in prayer with his Father God. He drew around him a circle of followers and laid the foundations for a separated group who were readily identifiable and came to be known as Christians. Their standards were not those of their day.

But on the other hand, it is to be noted that he did not choose to see his work develop in an isolated religious community similar to others that did exist in the Palestinian hills in his own day. He was out on the roads of Judea, on the populous city streets, along the lakeshores where people lived and worked. He did not even separate himself from sinners. Remember how he ate with them (Matthew 9:10-13). He spent time talking with them. He lived intimately among them.

Little wonder then that we can expect to bump into God on the busy city street. We will find him at the bank, in the library, at the soda fountain, in the department store. We will find him between neighbors talking over the backyard fence. We will find him in the bars and pool halls, in the hospitals, in the suburbs, in the hippie communes—wherever people are, and especially where people have problems.

The traditional American Protestant devotion to the separation of Church and State seems to be a valid principle. Certainly we don't want our faith to come under the control of politicians, and we don't want a wealthy and powerful religious organization to take over and usurp privileges of government in a free, pluralistic society. And yet devotion to this principle, valid as it seems to be, can encourage some mistaken notions about God. It can appear to say that there should be a separation between God and State. It can say that all of life is divided into absolutely separate spheres, one with government in it and the other with church in it. It can suggest that between these two stands a wall so high that not even God himself can scale it. Such may lead to an awkward and strange isolation.

For God and his faith support a wholeness within individual persons and a wholeness in life that should not be chopped up by fences such as we find here. Keep organized church and organized state separate, but remember that a whole God seeks to minister to the whole lives of people.

God is concerned with the affairs of State. He may work through government, through laws that are passed, and the ways they are enforced. He may work through the course of history that a country follows. It's not surprising, for most of us who are American Christians, to find him at work in our country. After all, it was established on principles that have their roots in the Christian tradition. Here is the high value placed on man, his freedom, his personal rights, his concerns for the welfare of the whole. Here is democracy, which finds some of its roots in the Judeo-Christian heritage.

But God in Communist China, where Christian religion is actively opposed? where there has been no long Christian tradition to start with? where men we regard as malevolent toward an orderly world society rule? That is harder to imagine.

God deeply involved in a small southeast Asian country full of poverty, disease, ignorance, and again with a "foreign" religion? Hard to imagine. But sometimes American Christians are guilty of putting a box around God and assuming whatever our national purposes are, whatever will work for the good of our nation, whatever we do "in the name of God," that is peculiarly on God's side. It may not always be so, for God is bigger than any national purpose. And the loyalty we owe him surpasses any other loyalty we may have.

It is easier for most of us to think of God when we are with a family, perhaps celebrating Christmas in pleasant middle-class surroundings in a small town or suburban setting. There is something that seems to many of us peculiarly hospitable to God in a green lawn and a white clapboard house, in an open fireplace, and at a dinner table heavily laden with the turkey and trimmings of an American Thanksgiving dinner. And certainly it is good if we sense God's presence there. But that may not really be his special dwelling place.

He may just as readily dwell—maybe more so—deep in an Alsatian coal mine or in a small village in Bulgaria behind the Iron Curtain, or at the meeting of a tribal organization in a young African country. It may be in an East Harlem tenement, or in the upper-crust affluence of a Scottsdale, Arizona, or among the shacks of a Mexican barrio.

32

What all of this really is saying is that, for God, the world is in a sense his home. He feels at home in every part of it because he is most at home meeting need and confronting problems. And we may be most at home with God, if we are working on political problems up to our elbows, if we are seeking to heal social problems with all our might, if we are living life alongside the rest of the people of the world, in sympathy with them, hearing and listening. God does not wear his robes of righteousness tightly around him, nor should those who bear his name. The righteousness emerges not in robes but in quiet commitment and in appropriate dedicated action.

The God we bump into is not too nice to be with us or with the dirtiest, most uncouth, most filthy looking and filthy minded reprobate you can imagine. God is not too nice to get dirty or sweaty or all caught up in the problems of the world. He's rugged and strong, this God we bump into.

THINKING THINGS THROUGH

Some Goals

To understand that God tangles with the world, is deeply involved with it, does not draw apart from it. To understand that the Christian response here would be like God's own. To explore the sphere of God's operations as being the world and all that goes into it. To move past a "nice," neat, little religion to one that is worthy of the strength and concern and deep involvement of God himself.

Some Questions to Consider

1. How deeply involved in political parties and specific political programs can Christians get and still give God priority in their lives? What about the church and church agencies themselves—can they get directly involved in political issues?

2. Is it better to continue offering prayers at community and political gatherings in the hope that these will remind

some people of God or is there more to be lost through casual immunization of people with a tiny bit of religion?

3. Are there times when a holy God will withdraw from something that is so evil, so antagonistic to the forces of good that it would be useless for him to stay related to it anymore?

4. In what sense is God present in bars, slums, hippie communes, crime syndicate headquarters?

5. How does a person make a public Christian witness and still avoid a holier-than-thou appearance?

6. How can typical religious observances—public invocations, table graces, even routine worship activities—be made to carry real religious meaning?

7. Is anyone really free of hypocrisy? Why or why not?

8. Where is it most easy for you to sense God's presence? Why is this? How does this fit in with what you have read in this chapter about God's presence elsewhere?

Some Things to Do

1. Go on a field trip through your community. Pray with your eyes open in neighborhoods where there are obvious social problems. Develop a worship service that moves along with you as you go.

2. Interview a Christian social worker, a Christian politician, a Christian law officer. Find out how they feel God is involved in their work. Find out if they ever worship while in the midst of a pressing problem related to their profession.

3. What does the Bible mean when it urges us to be in the world but not of it? Make a study in depth of John 17:11-16 using Bible dictionaries, commentaries, various translations. Discuss this with others.

4. Offer a prayer to God as God of the world and in it.

3

"Haven't I Met You Somewhere Before?"

Maybe God simply reminds us of somebody.
Maybe it is our father.

THROUGH GOD THE FATHER

After all, "father" is one of the most common figures
of speech we have to help us try to understand God. It
comes to us straight out of the Bible and especially from
the teachings of Jesus himself. He prayed to "our Father"
(Matthew 6:9). He mentioned that God cares for us just
as a good father gives good things to his children (Matthew 7:11). It is a figure of speech we have become comfortable with across centuries of the Christian faith.

But, wait a minute. Like any other good title, any good
figure of speech, father has its limitations.

Perhaps you have been teaching children. In the process
you may have discussed how God is like a kind, heavenly
father to us. You and the class may have prayed, "Our
Father, who art in heaven." And after you have done this,
you have looked deep into the eyes of one of the children,
and there you have seen some mixture of confusion, fear,
maybe even hate.

And then you have remembered. This child's father is
not a good example. The man beats his wife. He probably
has beaten this child. He goes off on drunken sprees. He

is coarse, uncouth, cruel. He does not have the respect of his family, neighbors, or any who know him. And yet this is the father this child knows best. No wonder this child is troubled when you talk about God as father.

The title Father comes to us in the framework of whatever cultural patterns are associated with the term. For many people, a father is primarily an authority figure. They remember a stern father or grandfather out of their childhood. He was the dictatorial head of the house. He brooked no opposition. He allowed no democracy in the family. He had to give permission for everything that was done. The whole family was dependent upon him to earn the family's living, to dispense the money, to okay purchases, to approve whatever activities came along. The term, therefore, can communicate the authority of God but perhaps in an overly harsh, dictatorial way.

Or maybe the image of father someone else has is a weak one. Maybe he is seen like the fathers in many television comedies. Maybe he bumbles like a Dagwood. Maybe he is henpecked, weak, shallow. The women's liberation movement might object to God being so exclusively understood under a male title. The possibilities for distortion in the father idea of God are, as you can see, endless.

Therefore, do we give up on this figure of speech? Do we no longer talk about God as father when we teach a class or discuss God with our children? A good many theologians of the last generation have been doing just that. They have given up on the father image of God for some of the reasons just listed or for others. For some of them this gives too personal an image to God, for example.

But fathers are portrayed as good in much of Bible teaching. They are intended to be good in God's plan for families, in God's calling to men to play their appropriate roles in families. Jesus taught us about a father God. So why not rescue the term?

36

Just because some men have distorted the image of father doesn't need to mean we give up on it. Good and wise people can redeem the image of father. Those fathers who are kind to their children, open toward them, democratic in family living, wise in their sensitivities to each child and to the mother—such can bring renewed meaning to the term.

The father image often is limited to the old-fashioned, authoritarian father we mentioned. In an earlier day fathers dispensed authority to young children, and then often died or otherwise moved out of the scene as their children grew to maturity.

But there is something beautiful in the picture, Gabriel Fackre reminds us, as we see a father across the years. He tenderly holds his infant child in his arms, communicating love through his strength and touch and active support. He guides and makes suggestions to the family as it grows in a democratic framework. There is guidance and authority here for the young child.

But as the child grows and comes of age, it is beautiful also to see the father gradually loosening the ties of control. It is a wonderful thing to see the flowering of young lives as they reach new areas of responsible freedom. The father in his wisdom knows just how to encourage the child to launch out on his own as he learns to use the freedom his father has given him. Then a new relationship with the father develops as the child matures.

Eventually the child comes to know this other person not just as a fatherly authority figure but as a friend. With his greater maturity, the child still finds things to learn from the father, but there is a new and growing sense of comradeship. Love deepens. Personalities blossom. Thus it is with the wise father as the years pass. The child has come of age and finds himself in a new, rich relationship with the father, who now is Friend, Companion, Elder Statesman, Counselor.

THROUGH JESUS CHRIST

Maybe we did meet God somewhere before—maybe it was through a young man who lived in Nazareth and taught at Jerusalem and other points around the east end of the Mediterranean Sea some two thousand years. This was the man called Jesus the Christ, called by some Master, by some Savior, by some the Son of God.

Certainly, according to what he said and by what his followers have said about him, he did come to show us God. It is said that he did this by his teachings, by his example, by the great and overwhelming events through which he lived. And so in his steps have come millions upon millions of persons who have found the deepest meaning of their lives in the company of those who name Jesus Christ as Lord, who through him have found God to be their loving father.

Of course, getting to know God has not always been easy for some people to manage through this channel. Jesus was, after all, a man who lived a long time ago. His teachings, while clear to some, have been misunderstood by others. God has sometimes lost something in the process of being communicated about by others across the intervening years.

For instance, he has been made to appear in a too-limited way by some of the artists, particularly by some of the medieval artists and the postermakers of the nineteenth century where he was painted with pale skin, fair ringlets, and light blue eyes. He has cometimes been portrayed in song and story as the "gentle Jesus meek and mild" rather than the vigorous Semitic teacher with strong, new ideas. Well-intentioned, creative persons forgot his historic origins, sought to make him most attractive to Europeans and Americans of nordic ancestry, sought worthily to make him appealing to little children.

But this has created a false impression that has turned off people from other places around the world—Africans, Asians, South Sea Islanders. It has sometimes disenchanted vigorous men and idealistic, discontented youth. In reality, Jesus was a man's man—as well as a man for women and children. He was more than a man of sentimentality. He was more than gentle. He was more than kind. Those things, of course, but also strength and toughness to meet hard situations.

Another thing that gets in the way is the impression of Jesus Christ as long ago and far away. Here was a man of oriental background, desert costume, long hair (until recently a foreign thing to our generation). His culture was strange to ours, his time in history two thousand years ago. His words come to us through translation and echo across all those years. His relevance to our time has not always been clear—perhaps it is to you and to me, but not to so many people who need to know him most urgently. He spoke about shepherds and sheep and village wells— which many people in our day have never seen close at hand. He lived in the open and often in rural situations— far different from our increasingly urbanized and suburbanized society. He walked where he was going, in contrast to our society centered in mechanized transportation. Long ago and faraway, so it seems to some.

Other distortions enter the picture. Some people take a magical view toward Jesus and forget his human side. They see him as an ethereal being, a ghostly kind of supernatural creature who indeed walked on earth long ago but who didn't really suffer the pains and undergo the hardships of a real man. They read how he went around performing miracles and figure that if he had any needs or got into any tight spot some kind of special miracle was going to sustain him. Since he was divine, they somehow feel, he never would have been tangled up in the troubles that our humanness gets us into—disease, deep pangs of hunger, loss of a sense of personal worth in the midst of poverty, sexual hangups, bothersome human weaknesses like jealousy, self-centeredness, lack of discipline, lack of purpose, envy, a whole range of things that erode the human spirit.

Actually, this view of Jesus was an early heresy in the church. It came early and sticks around pretty closely either out in the open or in the half-thought-through, scarcely realized attitudes that we may hold toward the Christ. These early persons who misconstrued the person they were ready to worship in Jesus were influenced in part by the Gnostics, Plato, and others who thought that the "flesh," the body, is evil. Therefore, how could Jesus, who is divine, have actually lived in "sinful" flesh? They assumed that what looked like a body to those around him must have been an illusion, not the real stuff.

Such a view deprives us of understanding Jesus whole. It makes an artificial separation between his spirit (divine) and the human flesh (sinful). It fails to take into account what God was trying to do when he showed himself to us through Jesus Christ—bridging the gap completely between the divine and the human, so that Jesus was totally divine but at the same time totally human in one indivisible, whole being.

At the other end of the scale of distortions of Jesus is the view that he was human and no more than that. Here indeed was a great man, some say, perhaps the greatest man who ever lived. Here certainly was a great and skillful teacher, perhaps the most compelling and insightful ever to offer his views in the marketplace of the world's ideas. Here was a man who, though limited in the number of people he actually met, never traveling more than a few hundred miles, had the strength of personality and the strength of ideas to establish a following that multiplied and grew across the centuries. Many people are vastly attracted to this human Jesus. They are almost ready to bow down and worship him while at the same time insisting that he was not truly God.

Just as in the case of God the Father himself no array of arguments is likely to persuade a person without faith to believe that Jesus was more than a great man. Those who believe that he was the Christ point to the miracles that it is recorded he performed, to the healings. The skeptics respond that many sorcerers and tricksters across the centuries have been credited with performing miracles and healings. Those who believe in the Christ point to his widely witnessed death and resurrection and later ascension. This is central in all Christian faith.

The skeptics feel that the record is not absolutely to be proved from this time and distance. Followers of the Christ point to the power of his teachings which have gained adherents in ever widening circles, that have attracted disciples even unto death. They place some trust in the wisdom of great men and women who have testified to Christ and his power across the centuries. Believers in the Christ point to how he fulfilled prophecy from the Old Testament.

All of these support the faith of those who believe that Christ was himself the unique Son of God. This was he who "emptied himself, taking the form of a servant, being born in the likeness of men. And being found in human form he humbled himself, and became obedient unto death" (Phil. 2:7-8).

Just as in the case of belief in God himself, however, the final evidence rests on one's personal faith in Christ. A personal relationship with the living Jesus is ultimately what proves or disapproves the divinity of Christ for a given person. This was what Paul experienced on the Damascus Road (Acts 9). Once you feel his saving power, his personal love, the shining pull of his claims on your life, then you know that Jesus Christ is Lord. The rational arguments for and against don't really supply the answer though they may point the way.

Let's move now beyond these issues that sometimes distort the ideas of Jesus Christ to some of the positive contributions Christ makes to our understanding of God.

Jesus provides us with a reference point in history when God came into the world, gave himself to it, acted in it, bridged the gap between divine and human. God is a God of history—and in that term· we sum up his actions in relation to the course of human events past, present, and future. The birth, life, teachings, death, resurrection, and ascension of Jesus Christ are historical events that demonstrate God's action in the world, God's concern with us and the course of history we follow. He demonstrates that indeed God is best met and understood at those points where man meets man, where man meets God in the stage of life as it is being lived out, event after event, day after day in this world of time.

Jesus contributes to our understanding of God through his direct teachings. While his teachings are consistent with the development of Jewish thought that had gone before him, he brought new insight and new emphases. The picture of God as a mighty tribal warrior who protected and rewarded and punished his people and was a great God among many gods is given a new look in the teachings of Jesus. The law of love replaces legal technicalities. God is made more intimate through Jesus' stress on him as heavenly Father.

The relationship shows up in simple, down-to-earth human terms: vine and branches, shepherd and sheep, groom and bride and bridesmaids. Living with a plus gets a push—going the second mile (Matthew 5:41), turning the other cheek. The internal attitude gets placed in the spotlight: Hate can be like murder (1 John 3:15). Sham is no good. Mere religious exercise is not enough. So the New Testament teaches us about God. In Jesus' teachings, brought down to us through the written word, the man of faith finds his most clear and dependable picture of what God is like.

Jesus also reveals God to us through his example. He leads a life of love and concern for others. He helps us understand what an important matter living as a servant rather than as a person to be served really is. He is, as Dietrich Bonhoeffer so compellingly stated it, the Man for Others. Here was the first truly unselfish man. Here was the man who was ready to die for us that we might find eternal life. This was the man who conquered death in this cause. Here was the man who brought us the clues to salvation, personally and as groups of people.

It was no accident that the central message of the early church, the message that won people to the faith by tens and thousands, was a simple recounting of Jesus' birth, life, teachings, death, and resurrection. It was a compelling example.

At the heart of it all is the conviction Christians hold about Jesus—that he is God on earth, in real life, in the flesh. He puts the face on the infinite God. He puts the hands of service and personal concern on the God idea. He puts the personal warmth and love that is God's into the picture where we can read about it and feel it in terms of one person to another. At the heart of it is the conviction Christians have that Jesus came to bring God's salvation to mankind. No wonder John 3:16 is so familiar and so beloved: "For God so loved the world that he gave his only Son, that whoever believes in him should not perish but have eternal life."

We are so caught up in the web of selfishness, alienation from others and from God, so full of rebellion that we can't find our own way out. Sin has a strong hold. Jesus came with that helping hand, acting as God himself would in the world. Through him, through his death and resurrection, we find that way out. We inherit eternal life. Again, it is a process that cannot be proved to the skeptic. It comes through an experience of personal relationship. But it is an experience which falls within the grasp of the most humble, uneducated, and simple of persons as well as the most sophisticated.

Those who these days most successfully bridge that two thousand years back to Jesus of Nazareth are those who have been caught up by and live in his spirit. They know and seek to live by his teachings. They have captured his style of servant living as they turn their lives into ones of helping. They feel his teaching and witnessing approach to other people and they carry it out through the example of their own lives and through the words they find to speak of him. And through Jesus of Nazareth, the Christ, the Savior, the Master Teacher, they have come in a unique and preeminently satisfying way to know the great God of the universe who battles evil and defeats sin.

THROUGH GOD THE SPIRIT

Maybe we met God somewhere before—only it was through the Holy Spirit. Orthodox Christianity insists that it experiences God through the Trinity. The great historic church councils were hard on those who felt that they understood God in other ways. These maverick views go off in a number of different directions. It all adds up to the kind of problem we are not likely to solve adequately for many people in the scope of this brief study.

Part of the problem is one of logic: How can a Christian insist that there is but one God but at the same time insist that there are three separate persons in the Trinity. Some have tried to solve it by saying that, one after another,

God takes on different roles. At one time he is playing the part of the father God on high. Such he was doing during Old Testament days. At another time, during the time when Jesus was on earth, he was playing the part of Jesus Christ, visible Man-God. And then later he moves to the role of the Holy Spirit as God present with us now in spirit.

The orthodox person questions this sequential sort of thing as he recalls Jesus praying to God on high while here on earth ("our Father, who art in heaven"). The Father and the Son must both have existed at that time. And then there are also references to the Holy Spirit in Old Testament literature. So it must not be neatly chronological.

Some people would reduce the Trinity to an analogy like this. Maybe God is like water. Only H_2O comes in different forms and is experienced by us in different ways. Soft, liquid water sometimes becomes concretized into a bodily form like ice, in much the same way as Jesus came into the world. At other times water becomes steam or vapor, almost invisible, much as the Holy Spirit comes into our lives. But it is all water. We simply experience water in different ways, and the Trinity then is seen by some as a figure of speech, even a poetic way or a literary device for helping us understand more fully the multifaced and complex God we serve. But no analogy can be fully satisfactory.

Others insist on finding a kind of hierarchy in the Trinity. The great God above is the central figure. Jesus as the son is a lesser being, as is the Holy Spirit. In fact in this view Jesus may have just a trace of derived or rubbed-off divinity in him.

Of each member of the Trinity, the experience of the church has had the hardest time to find a place for a separate and unique Holy Spirit. After all, God is spirit, and what is different about the Holy Ghost from the infinite God, who is Spirit himself?

45

And what special work, parallel to Christ's, does the Spirit have to accomplish? Jesus taught considerably about the coming of a Counselor or Comforter (one who would help us be strong by being present with us). An example of this comes in John 14:15-16. This and other teachings from the Bible indicate that there is special work for God-present-with-us in the spirit: Giving us special strength. Guiding us. Giving and helping us develop special gifts. Cleansing us of the guilt of sin. Giving us insight as we study the scripture, as we pray and meditate. Carrying on the work that Christ started.

But the Holy Spirit is hard to nail down. You can't put the Spirit in a neat formula or recipe and figure out exactly how he is going to work. Or he may be misinterpreted. Thus controversies get started about evidences for the presence of the Holy Spirit. Some people would argue that a person must speak in ecstatic or unknown tongues to show the presence of the Holy Spirit. Others are so repelled by that idea that they would find it difficult to fellowship with a person having such an experience and making such a claim. People entranced by the Holy Spirit idea sometimes wind up with vague, even very strange notions.

In spite of the confusions and distortions that exist here, we do find a basis for God ministering in the world today through his Holy Spirit. God is experienced by people as God-with-us, and operating in and through our lives. Whether this is God on high living here as spirit, the spirit of the resurrected and living Christ with us, or the Holy Spirit as separate personality among three, is not quite so important as the fact that God is indeed among us, according to the experience of relationship that people do have. Through the Holy Spirit we do come to know and experience God at work in our lives and in our world this very day.

It remains that people do meet and experience God in varying ways and that the idea of the Trinity helps us keep a balanced view toward God and an understanding of his ways. Some people have come up with the idea that God is faraway, distant, cold in his majesty. The idea of the Holy Spirit and Christ counteracts that. Others lose track of God's majesty, power, and overall kingship as they see him only as a close friend. The idea of the great God in the Trinity overrules that. Some people can understand God only through the historical event of a Son sent into the world. The idea of the Holy Spirit present with us now balances that.

THINKING THINGS THROUGH

Some Goals

To examine ways God reveals himself to us in a whole, comprehensive, and balanced way as Father God, as Jesus Christ, and as the Holy Spirit.

To find fresh meaning in the idea that God is like a Father.

To experience God directly and personally through the life and teachings of Jesus Christ and the present work of the Holy Spirit.

Some Questions to Consider

Consider the term *Father* as applied to God. What difficulties, if any, has this idea raised for you? What help does the term provide?

How does the present role of fathers in our society cause difficulty and give new meaning to the idea of God's being like a father?

What are some other terms that have meaning for you in describing what God himself is like?

If you were describing what Jesus of Nazareth looked like two thousand years ago, how would you picture him? If you were describing how Jesus might come to earth today, what would he look like now?

What do you think was the most important thing Jesus did and how did he do it?

If the only knowledge of God you have were to come through Jesus Christ himself, how might your picture of him be different from now?

What is your own explanation of the Trinity—how we believe in three persons in one Godhead?

What is the present work of the Holy Spirit?

Some Things to Do

Prepare a diagram (or several) you would use in trying to explain how God comes to us as a Trinity.

Make some posters carrying affirmations you would make about the God described in this chapter.

Recall important experiences you have had with God. What aspects of the Trinity seemed most important in these? Share.

Make a study of John 14, using commentaries, concordances, and various translations. What does this chapter tell us about ways God manifests himself?

4

"I've Been Reading about You"

You've read his biography.

You've seen him on television.

His name is in the papers all the time.

And finally you meet him. In person. Face to face.

Maybe he looks bigger or thinner or more handsome than the television tube pictured him. Maybe he seems kinder and more direct than the impression you gathered from the papers. But at any rate it's something like meeting an old friend when you finally run into someone you have read a lot about. Sometimes it can be that way with God. We may experience him personally and directly, but much of our understanding about God is shaped either directly or indirectly by the Bible.

HERE GOD REVEALS HIMSELF

While God is too big and comprehensive for us ever to understand fully he keeps trying to show himself to us. We consider some of these channels of self-disclosure in other chapters. We come to know him through his creation, through the way he works in history, through the ways he deals directly with people, and especially through his living Word: Jesus Christ.

But the backbone of all this revelation, that which we have with us now as a guideline, as a checkpoint, as a record of the way God has worked in special ways in history and through Jesus Christ is the written Word. The

Bible brings to us the ancient and extended account of how God dealt in history with the Hebrew people. In the Gospels we get a four-dimensional view of the ministry here on earth of his son Jesus Christ. In these pages we find the distilled wisdom of men closely in touch with God —prophets and poets, disciples and leaders of people, historians and letter writers.

And so in the sixty-six books written sometimes centuries apart in a variety of languages and literary styles, God comes through. While God's revelation is not limited to the pages of the Bible, there is really nothing else quite like it. It is unique. Here God has spoken so clearly through events, through psalms and words of wisdom, through letters, through history, that people across the centuries have found the pages of this collection of books speaking with strange power in their lives.

God led his people out of bondage in Egypt to the Promised Land. The record of this inspiring story forms a revelation of God himself. The Hebrew people carve out a land and nation of their own under the leadership of judges and kings. The record of how God dealt with his people in good times and bad has proved to be a revelation across the years as people turn the pages of Judges and 1 and 2 Kings. God worked mightily through the prophets; they gave him their ear, and he spoke through them. That comes echoing down through history as revelation through Isaiah and Micah and Hosea.

Jesus was born, taught, lived, healed, died on a cross, was resurrected, and ascended into heaven. Four Gospels bring to us even today that revelation of God through his Son. The early church grew and developed. It dealt with problems. Acts and the epistles bring this revelation. God gives strength to meet persecution and hard times as God's will unfolds, and this story comes to us through a work such as Revelation.

Among God's great acts in all of history has been his effort to reveal himself through a collection of writings we call the Bible. Without it we would be poverty stricken and our knowledge of God might be shallow, full of whim, and uncertain.

MEN WERE INSPIRED BY THE HOLY SPIRIT

Just as Christ has built a bridge between God and man in that he is both divine Son of God and a truly human Son of Man, so is the Bible a bridge between God and man in some of the same way. For it is a divine and human product, the result of cooperation of a special order between God and man. It is a divine-human book and reflects the qualities of both. These writers were inspired and partook of unusually deep religious insights.

Their work reflects both their humanity and their spiritual sensitivity. In this way we get a picture of their background, the situation out of which they wrote, and their purposes in writing. They reflect their human situation. Their own individual writing styles come through.

People think they find in Luke-Acts, for instance, all the signs that the writer was a physician. The Jewishness of the writer of the first gospel is evident. For the writer of the Fourth Gospel, the mastery of the common Greek of his day is a characteristic style and contrasts with the exuberant outpourings of Paul in his epistles. In these and other ways the humanness of the writers comes through, proclaiming to us in itself that God does break through into history to deal with human people. One of the places they meet is in the Bible itself.

God reveals himself, and he inspires men and women who respond to him. In this way inspiration came to the Bible writers. God gave them a divine message, a revelation, and as best they could in their human condition they wrote it down. They were inspired. Their words in turn have inspired readers and hearers of the written Word across the centuries since then. The validity of the revelation and the height of the inspiration have been proved continuously in the lives of people. The Bible has stood the test of time.

IT WAS HANDED DOWN TO US

The Bible, of course, doesn't come to us with the instantaneousness of our evening television news shows. It doesn't come to us with the rapidity of the morning newspaper or the weekly magazine. It originated a long time ago, in a different language, in a different world of customs, experience, and understanding. Somehow it has to bridge that gap between today and an oriental, nomadic, and simple culture of two thousand and more years ago. That it does speak to us with so much meaning across these generation and culture and century gaps is in itself an authentication of its worth.

The fact remains that the Bible comes to us as a product not only of the original writers in their contact with God but of many other kinds of people across many years in their own relationships with God.

After the original writers wrote, somebody else had to find enough value in these writings to keep them and circulate them, for this was before the day when it was easy to roll cheap copies off a speeding printing press or a quick copying machine. Eventually, leaders of the church had to find sufficient value in the particular books we now have in our Bible to include them in an officially selected and circulated canon of holy writ. The church's experience with these books had been good. They had found God through them, and placing them on an official list was intended to distinguish them from other worthwhile or even erroneous writings that were also being circulated.

Across the years the Bible moved with the "people of the book" out to the frontiers of civilization. Along the way the original Greek and Semitic languages found their way into the Latin Vulgate, into German, and into various English translations. Each culture that came in contact with Christianity found its Book of books to be of such value that it had to be translated into the current language. Particularly was this true after the Protestant Reformation came along, stressing the need for each man to be able to read the Bible for himself and be his own interpreter of God's word through it.

So, time, culture, languages changed. The message remained the same, but each culture and each generation found new ways of communicating the words of the Bible and their revelation about God. Typographers, printers, translators, bookbinders, radio broadcasters, and many others all began to share in the responsibility of keeping God's written word current. Songwriters picked up the chain. Musicians such as Isaac Watts transformed the Psalms into meaningful hymns. People composed and acted out the Bible message through plays. Great works of music, *The Messiah* and Brahms' *Requiem* carried the message. From those pulpits dedicated to communicating a Bible message came this written word on wings of a man's voice.

Behind all these forms stood the written word with its unique way of testing, affirming, mediating, insights into God. It stands as a heritage of ours out of the past, but it also proves itself each day to be alive for the present.

AND SO WE READ THE BIBLE

The Bible is still selling well. Probably there are not many homes in the United States without one or more copies. In spite of the cracks about its being one of the least-read best sellers of all time, it is in fact still widely read and deeply loved. Would only that it were more widely read, more seriously studied, and more relevantly put into practice in all areas of life.

53

In a class I recently asked the group to report on how they come at the Bible. This informal poll turned up the following approaches. You may want to consider how you fit into the picture.

1. *Reading the Bible to Accompany Personal Devotions.* About 20 percent of the class said they had daily devotions in which they used the Bible. Most of these simply looked up the passages referred to in their daily devotional guide. They felt they were largely seeking inspiration, help for the day. Their approach was to think about these few verses, usually in light of the text matter written in the guide for the day. They felt this was a scattered kind of approach. Sometimes they had a pretty good idea of the context out of which the passage came, its original setting, and other background. But since their approach was largely to be inspirational, they didn't feel it was too important to take a careful, studious approach at this point.

Another part of the class—about 10 percent—said they read longer passages daily, or almost daily, within a devotional framework. Again they were not reading for any scholarly purpose, but largely to foster a devotional and prayerful undergirding for their day. They said they somehow felt closer to God in reading his written word. Some of these people were reading a chapter or two at a time, going consecutively through a book. But they were picking their books pretty much at random. One or two were seeking to read a chapter out of the Old Testament and a chapter out of the New Testament each day, moving consecutively through these two parts of the Bible.

2. *Reading the Bible on Occasions when Special Help Is Needed.* Almost 90 percent of the class indicated they do this kind of Bible reading. It was for them a way of calling in God for a special need. They felt that through their reading of Scripture they somehow came to an under-

standing of God's will for them. Sometimes they just began reading at random. At other times they used their general knowledge of the Bible or the help of a concordance to turn to passages they felt would be relevant.

A few class members admitted to looking up certain passages on occasions like this in order to deal with somebody they were having a religious discussion with. They may have wanted "proof" for an argument. They wanted to prove a point.

Most commonly, however, this use of the Bible came at times when special need for help was felt. Maybe the person was discouraged. Perhaps some illness had come to him or a member of his family. Perhaps a tragedy. Or maybe it was simply a feeling that had come over the person: I ought to be reading the Bible more; it would be good for me; and I do enjoy it. Perhaps a crisis had to be faced or a big problem dealt with. Through the Bible, God would come into the situation.

3. *Reading the Bible for Personal Study.* Two or three people in the class said they approach the Bible in the form of personal, systematic study. They were not carrying out any particular assignment. They had simply made it a habit to try to determine in a systematic way what the Bible really has to say. These people said they were interested in finding out the truth of the Christian life, understanding God's will for them, and so they had simply made it a habit to study God's written word. They found it rewarding.

These people tend to use various aids to Bible study. Concordances offer them clues to following through on ways the Bible deals with certain concepts. For instance, they might look up all the references to "belief," "believe," "faith," and "doubt," during one series of study. Perhaps they would use the cross references found in many editions of the Bible. They might study a personality in the Bible and all the references to him. Sometimes they would make a detailed study of a book, delving into its authorship, the place where it was written, the audience to whom it was addressed, the occasion that brought on its writing. They would make a study of the type of literature involved (narrative, poetry, prophecy, letter, and the like). Commentaries were frequently mentioned as aids to this kind of study. The opinions of an interpreter would add light to the reading, although some readers felt that if they turned to a commentary too early in the study process it might short-circuit their own grappling with a passage and make them dependent on this outside source.

The value of using different translations showed up in the discussion. None of these particular readers had a knowledge of Hebrew or Greek, but they did find new dimensions that helped their understanding of what the original message may have been about by comparing translations. These include both the authorized kinds of translations done by groups of scholars and those more free and individualistic translations done by translators working alone.

4. *Studying the Bible in Relation to Special Assignments.* Since my informal poll was taking place in an adult Sunday school class, we did not have many there who themselves were studying the Bible at that time in connection with a teaching assignment. But the possibility was mentioned. If a person is called on to lead a devotional period, plan a worship service, give a church talk, or teach a class, he may seriously explore a Bible passage in order to bring depth to his fulfillment of that assignment. Again he will use the study tools just mentioned in an effort to get at all possible dimensions of truth connected with a passage. It certainly is important to understand an isolated verse or group of verses in its larger setting and within the original purposes of the book of which it is a part.

It is important to understand poetry as poetry, a letter as a letter. It helps to know about the author and the people to whom he first wrote, all for the purpose of understanding what really was originally meant. And as one prepares to teach or lead others in the consideration of a passage, it is also vitally important to understand what this passage can mean in our lives today. Only as this process is prayerfully and systematically carried through in a disciplined way is God likely to be brought to the people in the most relevant ways.

One danger for those who work with the Bible in relation to preparing special teaching and other assignments is that the process may become just routine. They may concentrate so much on the letter that the spirit gets lost. Or, the person who picks out a verse here and a small section there as proof for a certain viewpoint also runs some risk of coming at the Bible in a less than fruitful way. Picking an isolated verse out of its context can mean that its true intention will be missed. It can be misunderstood unless seen in the whole direction of the book in which it appears or in light of the whole movement of biblical history. But through all such a process, whether the approach be chiefly for inspirational purposes or for a solid understanding of what was meant originally and what is being said for today, the person can open himself for God to speak to him.

5. *Studying the Bible in Company with Others.* For about half the class that was polled, group Bible study is one of their richest experiences in approaching the Bible. For these people this happens at certain times in their Sunday school classes, in prayer meeting studies, and in small quest and Bible study groups. Some remembered doing this kind of study in earlier years in their homes but were not doing it at the present time. There is something valuable in such group study where earnest and concerned

effort at understanding the Bible together—mind meeting mind—goes on. Here again various people can contribute as they bring in different translations. A wide variety of experience with the passage and with related life problems can be shared. Being together at a stated time and place provides group discipline to the undertaking.

Related here is the kind of group experience with the Bible that can come when the Bible is used well in the worship services of the church and when a passage is dealt with in depth and at length from the pulpit in expository preaching. Listen, for in such ways does God speak.

The Bible introduces us to God in a way that no other avenue of revelation does. The testimony of countless Christians today and across centuries is that here in the pages of the Bible we find special word from God, special word about God. It fits remarkably into our lives because it is not just a book of subject matter to be studied about. Instead it is a book that brings us God's word as this applies to human experience and as we find meaning and importance in the ongoing flow of life.

THINKING THINGS THROUGH

Some Goals

To consider how God reveals himself to us through the pages of the Bible.

To explore the meaning of revelation and inspiration, particularly as this relates to the writing, transmission, and current study of the Bible.

To engage in reading and study of the Bible with fresh awareness of God's speaking to our lives in this way.

Some Questions to Consider

1. Where would you put the Bible on a scale of importance as a means of revealing God? First? Below personal and direct encounter?

2. Some people feel that there is a difference between approaching the Bible for daily inspiration and for serious in-depth study. Do you agree? What are the implications of your feeling about this for the way most people do approach the Bible?

3. The chapter suggests that just as Jesus is fully human and fully divine, so the Bible offers evidence of being a human book as well as a divine book. What are ways that it shows its human quality that might actually strengthen the influence the Bible has for you?

Some Things to Do

1. Build a case for the Bible, using from the Bible itself some passages that emphasize its importance. In Luke 1:1-4, the writer sets forth his purposes. John gives a reason for writing in John 20:31. Paul expresses gratitude for the Scripture that preceded his work in Romans 15:4. The Psalms speak more generally about God's word: Psalms 19:8; 119:72, 82, 89, 103, 130. Other such passages: Acts 17:11; John 5:39; 1 John 5:13.

2. Take the poll of your class or of other people in your congregation about how they approach the Bible. Compare its results with those described under "And So We Read the Bible" in this chapter.

3. Set up a special Bible study and reading program which a group of persons agree to practice for one week. Discuss thoroughly in advance just how you will go about it. Then discuss the results a week later.

5

"H-h-how D-d-do You D-d-do, Sir!"

Sometimes I've wondered what I would do and say if I were suddenly thrown in with one of history's great leaders and had to make conversation with him for an hour or so. What would I say? What would I do? Would my tongue be tied in knots out of excitement or would it ramble on and on irresponsibly? What if the great one didn't like me? Would we have enough in common to talk about? Would I, a grown man, ask him for his autograph, and would he give it to me?

Americans, especially adolescent girls encountering matinee idols, or young boys meeting sports stars, are autograph hunters. It is a way of establishing a personal link with the great. It is a way of capturing a bit of that person to have and hold forever. People sometimes seek God's autograph, too. They may find it in meditating on a beautiful or wondrous part of creation which they attribute to a creator God. They may find it in historical events, where they see him at work, his purposes being carried out. They may find it in a personal experience where they can testify that God has touched their lives.

Some may be like the little girl-theologian who asked her daddy: "Is God in this town with us? Is God in this house with us? Is God in this room with us?"

"Yes, he is everywhere, and he is right here with us," her father replied.

"Is he right here in the air all around us?"

"Yes," said the father, growing now a little impatient as fathers do.

With that, the little girl suddenly clamped her hand over the glass sitting on the table and shouted gleefully, "I gotcha, God! I gotcha."

So it is that we seek to capture God and put him in a jar where we can display our possession of him and analyze and display him as we would any other possession. That is one extreme of the situation. The other is to feel that God, whoever or whatever this great force and bond of wholeness in the universe may be, is so great and so far removed from us that we dare not even think of approaching him closely or as person to Person. This is an image that inspires little more than awe, maybe even fear.

Our method on through this chapter will be to draw a line from the extremely close, personal, and immanent view of God in a number of areas on the one hand to the very impersonal, removed, and transcendent view of God on the other side. We have already looked at the more intimate and casual extremes in a previous chapter, and so our attention here will tend to be on the transcendent and awe-inspiring side.

The line we draw between the extremes may be regarded as a continuum on which you can place yourself at this moment. As you do this, there are a number of questions you might ask yourself. Does my feeling about where I am along this line between the two extremes vary from time to time, depending upon my mood? Why or why not? Is a continuum an accurate way to picture the situation, or if we were charting it would some other drawing be necessary to allow for more feelings about God's transcendence and immanence to exist simultaneously and side by side?

WHERE IS GOD?

		Far away, not
Here, in me		interested in
and a part of me	_____	me and my world

We have already seen some of the problems associated with confusing God and self, so close may we feel that God has come to us that we identify him with our own wishes and desires. At the other end of the spectrum is the view that God, whatever great personal or impersonal force he may be, at one time may have set in motion those forces that created our universe, but now he is no longer interested directly in us or our affairs. Deistic philosophy and religion, strong in many quarters at the time America was first taking shape, reflects this kind of view. It may allow for a highly ethical and advanced kind of society concerned about human rights. It may be very rational in appearance. But it does not breed a sense of close relationship with a God who is intimately interested in us and involved with us in our human predicament. It is a philosophical position that is eminently satisfying to some kinds of persons but not to most human beings.

Most people will put themselves somewhere along the line between these extremes. They experience God as something other and beyond themselves. They do see God as high and lifted up, great in his majesty and far beyond our pettiness. But they also experience him as being close at hand. They like to feel God with them and to understand him great enough to be the Lord of the far galaxies as well. Some see this as an effort to have your cookies and eat them too. Is there any problem here for you?

HOW PERSONAL IS GOD?

A person much		An impersonal
like man	_____	idea or force

This is one of the questions that has occupied philosophers and theologians with intensity in recent years. But it also has had its practical problems for the man on the street. Somehow a picture of God in the form of a man has come out. Many a child has grown up feeling that the church was teaching him about a God who mysteriously was a man upstairs somewhere. Maybe he looked something like the photographs of his own great-grandfather, a rather dignified and stern old gentleman. Or maybe he lingered in the shadows of the modern mind but looked something like those paintings of stern-visaged Old Testament prophets.

Such an image hasn't set well with modern man. Many a young person has reached adulthood, thinking himself pretty wise and wishing to get rid of the superstitions of his childhood. There in the attic of his mind he found this old picture of a God who looked like a man and acted like an antiquarian judge of some sort. The youth felt members of the Christian community gave him this picture and he disliked and distrusted them for it.

Now it's very likely the Christian community as a whole never really set out to give him that picture. But maybe somewhere along the line he had a friend, sat with a Sunday school teacher, or hatched out his own idea that God is like his great-grandfather and the teachings of the Christian community never got him straightened out on it. Maybe he saw some picture of an Old Testament prophet when he was too young to understand who was really being portrayed and he identified that with God. Or maybe he took the prissy pictures of a mild Jesus and confused those with God.

Perhaps he took literally, as small children are likely to do, some of the figures of speech that we toss around concerning God. We speak of God's face, his hands. We talk about his heart, his eyes, his ears. When used carefully they are simply figures of speech to refer to God as a person, but they are easily misunderstood to make God merely a man. This is the anthropomorphic view of God, and it is fostered by some poetry, some hymns, and some sermons. But it can mislead about what God really is and drives thinking moderns away from Christianity at that very point.

If some people mean that they want to get rid of the anthropomorphic view of God when they talk about the death of God in this sense, they have a point that is well taken by many young people and young adults these days. But these young men and women have been confused about what Christianity has actually been teaching. It is well to let the mere-man-image God die, for that is inadequate and misleading. God is infinite—so we are taught in the Bible by passages like John 1:18: "No one has ever seen God." That is an outright declaration that he is not finite, limited to a body and other characteristics associated with being human.

How, then, does this relate to understanding God as a person? It doesn't necessarily do away with God's being a person to stress that he is not finite, that he does not have a body, even a spiritualized body akin to ours.

But what do we mean by *person* in this sense? The Greeks, who had something to do with the way the New Testament describes persons, saw persons as a set of characteristics that identify a being as separate, individual, distinctive. Our idea of personality comes close to this. The identifiable role that an actor takes on in a play comes close to this. *Person* is an amalgamation of individual purposes, styles of life, ways of doing things. These have to be observable, identifiable. In this sense, does the man of faith understand God as person? He is at least that! This doesn't make him an embodied, finite God, which would be an unscriptural view. Nor does this leave him as an impersonal force, alone. Perhaps you would therefore place yourself at some point along the preceding continuum. God is a person, not a finite being on the one hand or an impersonal, vague oblong blob kind of idea on the other.

HOW DOES GOD RELATE TO US?

He has a sentimental, buddy-buddy kind of love for us.	He is the stern, unbending, blind judge.

Which will it be? The completely disinterested enforcer of natural law who in unbending style goes about his cold, distant business? Or, the sentimental lover of my soul who holds my hand? We have already discussed the latter. And our hunch was that most people, over the long run, feel uncomfortable with that kind of God.

But what good is the other extreme? You may find legitimate need for a sense of justice in our universe. You may observe the tracks of this kind of justice. The law of gravity gets enforced pretty uniformly against whoever disregards it. But then man learns some other things about the way nature works and he is able to beat gravity for a while with a gas balloon. He learns something else and he can work against it with the air foil of an airplane wing. A helicopter blade or a hovercraft may help him do it. So may a spacecraft. Then it becomes an accident when something goes wrong and once more the law of gravity comes fully into play.

But no one denies that injustice is left to run abroad in other areas in our life together in this world. Not always is the God of justice to be counted upon to change the picture. Ofttimes the wicked rich get richer. The righteous poor get poorer. Minority racial groups may grow more oppressed, and the God of justice is not seen doing his work. He must be disinterested indeed. Or his work may be thought to take place in some other dimension, in some future life. But the modern man of the world with his own keen sense of justice often is disappointed by what seems to come from the God of justice.

Somewhere in between these extremes in possible views of God comes a look at how God relates himself to us through the highest kind of love. Seen in the light of Jesus' teachings and as communicated to the early church by Paul, this love is an intelligent good will toward man. It is not moved around by the emotion of the moment even though it takes that into account. It is full of warmth and concern. It is not really a different breed of emotion than the passion two people may feel toward each other. Nor is it different from the philanthropy that wealthy people may display toward needy persons in their community. It combines the best in all this into a warm, intelligent, purposeful expression of the highest concern. It is made of sentiment, sympathy, and empathy, but it is not dominated by any of these. It is controlled by a wise sense of justice and is not isolated from it.

It is this which lies at the base of God's relationship with man. God in action has been called love himself. He exists at his very most meaningful place when he here comes into relationship with man. He exists most helpfully when one man has this kind of relationship with another. On the other hand God is more, of course, than love. All love is not God, but as 1 John 4:8 says God is love.

WHAT SHOULD BE OUR FEELINGS TOWARD GOD?
Passive   Utter
trust? _____ fear?

The extremes outlined here begin on the left with what is called passive trust. This is the kind of attitude that allows one to relax completely in acceptance of and dependence upon God. No more do we have to think or act. We can lie down in pleasant pastures of absolute trust in God, with no more intellectual battles.

On the other extreme comes an utter fear of God, even a sense of terror. Out there somewhere, it is feared, is the mighty, vastly just God who will punish like a despot when his slightest whim is crossed. He is great and majestic and distant. He was made to be feared and expects that from us. He inspires this fear, it is felt, so that we may be deterred from evil ways. His holy righteousness is so great and our human wormlike condition which leaves us groveling in the dust is so low that the only appropriate attitude as we look across the vast gap is to express our fear as we bow before his shining glory.

Obviously, a more comfortable and meaningful stance for man comes when we move away from these extremes. The passive trust is not appropriate for one created in the image of God with high and noble purposes. It does not allow us to be active and alive enough. It leaves us stupefied or in the state of the simplest animals. It does not leave us room to think, to go on intellectual pilgrimages. Even doubt is a tool here on the way from the passive state of absolute and blind trust to one of open-eyed, committed faith. The very idea of faith implies that we take a stance of commitment and obedience in the face of some possibilities of doubt. Faith involves us with active minds in search and active bodies in obedience to that to which we have given ourselves.

Nor does the role of utter fear seem appropriate for the man created in the image of God, assuming his love and concern for us. He would be embarrassed by our fearing attitude toward him. The Hebrews in the Old Testament really had a more moderate view of fearing when they understood that they were to fear God. This was holding him in awe because of his exalted place in the world. This was recognizing that, after all, he is God and we are men. This was worshiping him and giving him our loyal allegiance. This was obeying him, recognizing that to disobey would bring the fearful consequences of being out of harmony with the universe and the way it is meant to run.

So, fearing God in a biblical sense means moving away from the extreme suggested at the end of the line. The middle ground between the two could involve a number of other terms. Faith with the eyes wide open, not being afraid to use doubt as a means of groping toward new light, testing where we stand, feeding our discontent with the status quo, spurring growth in Christ. Commitment to God would be involved here. We believe in him and we think him worthy of our awe and self-giving as an object of our reverent respect; therefore, we commit ourselves to him. Hope could enter the picture somewhere along this line. We are forward-looking in our faith. God knows the end from the beginning. We are hopeful in our feeling of reverence for God. He is out there in the future and he will honor his commitments to us. Holding the future in his hands, he understands us and how we feel toward him from that perspective. Cross passive trust and fear and the far better result is the life of active faith and hope.

HOW SHALL WE EXPRESS OUR WORSHIP?

Passive as breathing?		Emphasis on exalted majesty?

Perhaps you are already thinking of times when worship meant the most to you. Perhaps it was a simple sense of God's presence in the face of some great crisis that came into your family. Perhaps you were stirred by the beauty of an oceanside sunset or the power of a mountain storm. Perhaps you worshiped most as someone you loved bowed at an altar of prayer to commit himself to God. Perhaps it came in a moment of silence at a simple service. Perhaps a chorus of fervent amens in response to a heartfelt sermon moved you. Perhaps you were most stirred by the singing of an unseen, huge choir, backed by the swelling tones of a great pipe organ.

Already, you see the direction of our thinking here. In contrast to some of the continuum lines, where the extremes do not seem like live options to modern man, perhaps here is an occasion where the whole range of options may suggest possible choices, either for different kinds of persons or for the same person in differing situations and with different needs. Yet, there is often an intolerance toward someone else's style of worship if it doesn't happen to fit in with what meets the taste and need of one individual. Whether a person kneels in a cathedral or by a farm bedstead, whether one sits silently in meditation in a plain meeting house or stands to sing with all the emotions pouring from his lungs—each may be the avenue that leads one into a sense of God's presence where he can express his awe and praise to God and receive assurance of forgiveness and guidance from him in return.

Perhaps this sums up what we have been saying about who God is on this scale of nearness to farness. For based on the experience of men in Bible history and more recent times, God cannot be nailed down to any one place on that continuum. He is both very near and very far. He is right here with us in our human situation, in every problem that faces us, and he is high and lifted up, the exalted ruler of the mountains, seas, skies, and stars. In that spirit we would worship him.

THINKING THINGS THROUGH

Some Goals

To think through how we can relate ourselves to the God who is both lovingly close at hand and majestically faraway.

To consider certain patterns of relationship depending on how personal we understand God to be, what our feelings toward him may be, where God's primary location in this world is.

Some Questions to Consider

How free, really, do you feel with God?

In what sense is God closer than breathing and high and lifted up? Do you think that God and a person can come so close together that God actually becomes a part of the person? In what sense can this happen? In what sense do you resist it?

After all, if this is helpful, what is the problem with envisioning God as like a person with a body?

How is God like a person to you? Do you have any problems with an understanding of God as a person?

What are the problems with having passive trust in God? complete fear?

What mood in worship means most to you, helps the presence of God seem most real?

Some Things to Do

Place yourself on the continuum lines that appear throughout this chapter as you feel right now. Consider how your feelings on this vary from time to time.

Transfer these continuum lines to large charts and get a number of people to place themselves on the continuum as they feel right now.

Write out for yourself your own feelings about how close to and how far from you God is at various times. Do you find a sense of direction or movement showing up here?

What differing views of God do we get in these Bible passages? Compare and contrast Isaiah 46 and Genesis 12:1-9; 28:10-22. Compare and contrast John 1 and Revelation 1.

6

"I Want to Ask You a Thing or Two"

For some people questions about God come most strongly into focus when one of these things happens:

A young mother suffers for months with cancer and finally dies an agonizing death. She leaves four small children and a grieving husband. Her aging grandmother, long senile and not able to care for herself, lives on and on.

Why?

Three thousand persons lose their lives in a Peruvian earthquake. Men, women, children—all are caught in this accident of nature.

Why?

A brilliant young man in college, sparkling athlete, campus leader with every prospect for a life of useful leadership, is struck by a drunken driver on a country road. The young man will be paralyzed from the neck down for the rest of his life.

Why?

A baby suffers brain damage at birth and will grow up mentally handicapped. She will be a burden to the spirits and financial resources of her parents who are spending their lives in committed Christian service.

Why?

A shrewd and crafty man buys up mortgages on property throughout his city. As one family after another comes upon hard days, suffers loss of employment or the death of the breadwinner, the man forecloses. He grows more and more wealthy each month, while those upon whom he feeds suffer with greater intensity.

Why?

The question is a persistent one across the recorded history of mankind. At the very moment of a crisis experience—death, natural calamity, the victory of evil, man is most aware that there is indeed something beyond himself. He may call this God, or a purpose in the universe, or whatever helps make sense out of it all. But what sense is there when evil triumphs, when suffering, tragedy, and death occur? Like Job we are faced with desperate questions here and we go on a quest for answers.

We can take various kinds of attitudes toward God in answer to this *why*. Let's look at some of them.

"GOD IS NOT AS STRONG AS THE POWER OF EVIL"

Some people figure that if God loves us and wants the best for us, then something must be keeping him from delivering all the time. Surely if God is good he must be frustrated when things don't go right for his people in the world. There must be a malevolent force that is working against him and a lot of the time is winning out. Maybe we can see good in the death of an elderly saint who has lived a full and rich life. He comes now to a final triumph if he can die in dignity and with some victory over the problems he has met during his life.

But often death doesn't come that way. There seems to be only tragedy in the death of the young mother. Or what good can there be in the death of hundreds by earthquake? Or how can a good God stand by while the Nazis kill Jews by the hundreds of thousands in the ovens of Dachau?

Or while a few wealthy, wicked men enrich themselves at the cost of life and well-being of hundreds of poor?

So some people look at the situation and figure that God must simply not be able to stand up in some way against the power of evil that must be the source of these troubles. Maybe, they say, he has limited himself in some way so that he cannot intervene in these situations.

Some people try to take a long view on this. They say that God must have decided to give the natural order as well as man some free rein if there is to be the free and voluntary association of love between God and man. This satisfies some. But others feel that surely God could have worked out this free fellowship business another way, as wise and strong as he must be, without opening the door for all this suffering, tragedy, and evil.

Still others do give high place to the power of evil. They find it in man. Or they may find it in a Satanic force itself. They externalize evil, put it out there where they can point their fingers at it, and say *that*—not God, not us—is the source of all our problems.

Maybe these are all battles between God and evil, and these skirmishes God has lost to the power of evil even while he works toward an ultimate victory.

No matter how you cut it, this view that strong evil is winning when suffering and death take place leaves God playing second fiddle to Satan.

"GOD DOESN'T CARE"

Another attitude we can take is that God doesn't care about the suffering and dying young mother. Here one assumes that God is busy with more important matters, maybe taking care of a star that's about to go astray out there in some distant galaxy. Or maybe you can assume that he set all the world in motion and now he's gone on vacation, or off in a laboratory keeping his eye on the dials, watching for the big problems.

A more sophisticated approach here is not to see God as loving, kind, warmly, intimately purposeful. In fact he may not be personal in his relationships to man at all. He may simply be that Ultimate Reality, a complex of final truth toward which science, philosophy, and religion all push. He may simply be a force that moves the world along. There may be a move toward order that holds things together in a reasonably systematic way despite the disruptions of natural calamity, evil, and suffering.

"GOD IS PUNISHING US, TRYING TO SAY SOMETHING TO US"

Here is a common view, and it has some support in common Jewish and Christian heritage. As Old Testament writers interpreted Hebrew history, for instance, we see this common rhythm: The Hebrews loved God, served him, obeyed his laws, and prospered. Their country would develop in power and influence. Then in the midst of affluence and power they would forget about God, begin to ignore his precepts. At this point the just God would step into punish, the Hebrews would be defeated in battle, and their national strength and prestige would decline.

It is easy to understand the chastising, disciplining hand of a father. It is easy to see how a just and righteous God might work for the discipline of his people. But, for many, it is hard still to understand the agonizing death of a young mother, perhaps a Christian, a devoted wife, an upright woman in every way. And even if she or someone near her were being punished by this painful death, such a death would work its own agony on innocent people around her—children, parents, husband. It is hard to find the justice in such a view of punishment through death and suffering.

True, a person may learn lessons through evil, suffering, and death around him. He may be reminded of his immortality, of his human, limited, rather dependent state.

But often the so-called punishment looks to be out of all proportion to any lesson to be learned, and the image of a just and loving God is lost in such a ghastly picture.

"THERE IS NO GOD"

In the face of these problems of human existence, some people may simply throw up their hands and say, there must not be any loving, kind God. If there is a God, they say, he must be vengeful, mean, and evil himself. How else could all of these ills take place in a world where God reigns? Just look at the world picture, these people say. Just see if it makes any sense to you that God is here and that he is kind and loving? While there is a measure of good in the world, fun, pleasure, happiness, everything is covered over with pain and hurt. Everywhere you look there is sorrow, tragedy, harshness.

Look at the basic harshness of nature itself. Plants spring up only to wither and die in heat and drought, only to be killed in the end by frost. One animal feeds upon another. Everywhere you run into natural catastrophes. The balance of life is so delicate here that only a slight misstep by man seems to throw it off. And out of all the universe, apparently only in the most limited of places, such as Planet Earth, are conditions mild enough to support human life. If any of this makes sense, it is said, in light of a loving God, it is not very apparent. So, it is charged, God either has malevolent purposes, no purposes for the good of man at all, or does not exist.

"GOD'S WAYS ARE MYSTERIOUS"

Some people admit the problems. But they also stick by the goodness of God. And they wind up appealing to man to have faith in God even though we can't understand his ways. There is a mystery here, they say. That satisfies some kinds of minds. It is enough for people of great faith. It is enough for others who are merely phlegmatic and don't want to wrestle with the issues. The resort to accepting all this as mystery is a way out of the dilemma and is satisfactory to many people.

But others cannot accept this, at least not all the way. Why, they say, should there have to be a mystery surrounding such crucial issues as these? They demand rational answers.

Perhaps some Christians too easily rely on this way out. "God's ways are past finding out," they say. "The man of faith and hope is willing to look beyond these persistent problems of evil and hope to understand it all better some day in the future. Don't doubt God; just accept his promises." Such views have their place, but it remains that the appeal to mystery and future unraveling of the mystery leaves many kinds of people completely unsatisfied.

"WE ARE BLINDED BY OUR HUMAN SITUATION, BUT GOD HAS PERSPECTIVE"

This is the Little-Old-Philosopher's stance on such issues, and along with viewpoints in some of these other paragraphs he has something going for him here. This view says that we don't stand where God stands. We have only our limited, human perspective. What looks like tragedy to us, caught here in a moment in eternity and on one tiny speck in the universe, may not look that way from God's timeless, limitless view. Death opens the doors to something so much more wonderful in the light of eternity that no death is really tragic, this outlook says. Any momentary suffering or discomfort is such a piddling thing in light of God's greater and more glorious plans for his people that these are just passing instants that may help discipline and guide us.

Another Little-Old-Philosopher view here is that for man to know what joy is, he must experience some sorrow. For him to understand even a little about life, he must see or experience death. Before he can measure the heights of victorious living he must experience the depths of tragedy. The view says that opposites are needed to help define each other. But again the doubters wonder about such views. Why in a powerful God's scheme of things would such opposites be necessary? Couldn't he work around such things? Even a parent with all his human limitations is not going to inflict pain on his child deliberately and severely as fate sometimes does, in order that the child may have all the greater joy when the source of pain is taken away.

NOW THAT WE'VE PAINTED OURSELVES INTO THIS CORNER, WHAT?

So here are a half-dozen ways people respond to questions about God when faced with the problems of evil, death, and suffering. Maybe you noticed at once that some of these solutions appeal to you and some don't. Maybe you've decided that you don't stand entirely in any one of these camps. Perhaps you have shifting feelings here, are sometimes sure, sometimes uncertain. As a matter of fact this points up the complexity of what faces most people. We are not dealing here with a simple problem that has, for most people, a simple answer.

The problem of why evil, suffering, and death exist in the same world with a loving, kind and good God constitutes what is often referred to as a persistent life issue for people. The questions in some form first occur among children at the very dawn of their conscious thought processes. They persist in varying forms for people on through youth, middle years, and into old age. They come to us in varying ways and get "answered" in varying ways. Perhaps the childhood answer is outgrown, and it all re-emerges for a youth. Perhaps it all seems settled for a young adult only to get torn up again when that person a few years later faces some new tragedy.

It is perhaps helpful, then, to see this family of questions related to God for what it is: a complex and persistent issue. It will not be answered for most people in a simple, once-and-for-all way. So instead of precise answers, we are perhaps better off to seek a style of living or a way of standing in the face of these questions rather than too-neat answers that may crumble out from under us at the next ring of the telephone with bad news or the next catastrophic headline. Just what can our style of response or our stand consist of?

1. *We can admit, realize fully that we live in a changing, dynamic world that is not neatly and perfectly wrapped up.* It has its imperfections. Nature itself as best we can observe it is not perfect. It has its ragged, loose edges. Man was not created perfect and the society he has developed has its injustices, inconsistencies, and evils. From our human standpoint we simply have to recognize that there is Satanic force at work in the world. This crops up in human behavior. One man is malicious, hateful, hurting others. Whole nations become instruments of evil power. Imperfection and evil are a reality.

Fortunately, under God, there are some things we can do about evil and imperfections. Don't let me give a too-simple view here, but within our human limitations and despite our mistakes and inertia, there are things that we can do. God has given us the gift of growth. Growth in right directions can be an answer to evil and imperfection. God, through Jesus Christ, has given us salvation. Our lives can be turned around. Problems in our society can be corrected as we come within the will of God. God has given us skills, capacities, insights, muscles with which to work. Our activity can lead us to do something about evils.

Not every wrong not every sorrow in our world can be traced to something evil, something imperfect in our world about which we can do something. But remarkably large numbers of these things do lie within some kind of control of man. And things are being done. One after another, diseases that have caused sorrow, sickness, suffering, and death are being conquered. Our conscience on social ills grows more sensitive, and now and then headway is made.

We are learning how to build highways and automobiles that are safer. We learn about fire prevention. Some of the world's causes of suffering and death lie within the potential control of our hands. Certainly, here is one of the stances we can take toward evil and suffering. They so frequently result from our carelessness, ignorance, evil, and imperfectness. And when that is the case, there are things we can do.

2. *We can take an understanding, in-tune attitude toward life as it is.* This accepting attitude admits these problems in life as it is. It doesn't blame God, but it doesn't rule him out of the picture either. It doesn't simply try to explain things away. It does figure we may learn more and understand more about reasons for tragedy later.

This is the attitude that accepts the human position where we don't have full perspective and understanding of everything. It may say that because of the evil around we can better understand the good. It says we may need the chastening and discipline of some pain for our own good. That same suffering may be needed to help us appreciate joy and pleasure fully. Of course, as we have already mentioned, these may be argued against. But the stance that is suggested here is simply one of accepting. And accepting is possible for people of some temperaments throughout their lives and for other people at certain moments. This does not claim to be a whole answer, but it does suggest itself as a helpful way to live out lives reasonably in a world where evil and suffering are realities.

Here the man of faith in God can take such a stand, trusting God to help him through the situation, to give him the strength that he needs. All around us are examples of noble and strong people who have borne great sorrow and pain and tragedy nobly with the help of faith in God.

3. *We can understand that to be human blends persistent pain with persistent joy and wonder.* This is closely related to the stance just described. Just as our Savior himself was a man of sorrows and acquainted with grief (Isaiah 53), so that seems to be the lot of the human being. It is in a way a gift, for there is an exquisite quality and depth of life that comes with sensing sorrow, experiencing in common with our fellowmen and with Christ himself the pain of being human. It is a pain that grows out of a sense of our limitations, out of our sympathies and concerns for others, out of having sensitivities that pick up whatever is going on both joy and sorrow.

Joy and sorrow are kin. The line between them can get pretty fine. The person who is most fully alive, most alert, most active, most deeply involved in life is going to feel more of both than the person who builds walls around himself, who crawls into a shell, who is so afraid of life that he does little more than sleep his way through it. Take the Kennedy family, for instance. This family literally threw itself into life. It produced a president and senators, national leaders. Always traveling, always active in sports, deeply enjoying life, doing things, perhaps making mistakes along with right choices, life was there to the full. It brought high risks toward both joy and sorrow, and the family experienced both in full measure.

Again, this view of what it means to be human doesn't answer to many of the questions about evil and suffering. Certainly not for all people. But it does suggest an outlook to be taken, an understanding of ourselves that may be helpful, in the face of them. This is the way, it seems, God has made us, and if it can be accepted we are on the road to abundant living.

4. *We can respond to the question of evil and suffering with trust that God is good and does love us, with faith that he will strengthen us for any trouble evil and suffering bring, that there is purpose and reason in the midst of this and hope for a better day.* At first glance this does not look like a very intellectual answer to our problem with evil and suffering. And perhaps it isn't. Perhaps it is not a response immediately within the grasp of all. Some people have too much native or learned skepticism for this. Some people need to have things wrapped up more neatly.

The fact remains that there is much mystery and much that cannot be dealt with on an intellectual basis about this whole matter of evil and death in relation to God. The God of my faith looks with favor upon persons with their honest doubts. He sees doubt as part of the best kind of pilgrimage leading at last to faith. For doubt is a spur to exploration and to discovery. It is a key step on the road for many a young person in the process of moving away from a secondhand religion he has received from his parents to a vital, firsthand faith of his own.

Faith and hope are not just last-resort attitudes that weak people finally latch on to when their intellectual powers give out. For many they come as one person experiences another. You get to know a neighbor casually. Over a period of time you meet and talk with and work alongside that man. You get to know him and he knows you. You find out the ways you can trust him. You gain faith in his integrity. The man of faith bumps into this Other, this God, and he feels a personal relationship developing. It becomes a matter of trust. It is strong. It is not something to be proved, to be argued about. He simply accepts the relationship and what he has is faith.

Particularly when it comes to questions like evil, death, and sorrow in the midst of the faith relationship, there is a string of expectation that ties it all together. It is faith not just for the here and now but also for the future. Hope gets involved. Hope says that evil will be dealt with. Hope says that death when it comes will be good for the person involved and that it opens the door to a glorious and victorious life beyond. Hope says that in humdrum and discouragement, in the sorrow and pain of the here and now, there is an overriding purpose that moves and makes progress. Hope says that, this all adds up to a quality of life that is rich and full of meaning, joy and wonder.

This response will not lose track of the idea that God is a God of justice in the midst of these situations. Basically that is good news. It means that he has concern for order. It means he will be fair. It means that he will make room for love to operate as a drive toward change for the good of people. But in the exercise of his justice, some judgments are going to be rendered that aren't just sweetness and light. As a man whirls down a twisting mountain road at eighty miles an hour, drunk, bleary-eyed, the natural order of things, reflecting God's judgment, is likely to apply. The tragedy in this—a persistent issue that stays with us—is that others may be hurt, too.

5. *We can respond out of a kind of "divine discontent."* We are unhappy with many things as they are, just as Jesus was discontented with the world into which he came. We want to defeat evil. We want to change things that are wrong. The Christian hardly dare take his ease in Zion when so much is troubled and upset in our society. In this dynamic, changing situation might it be possible that we would sometimes find ourselves on the side of those who cannot accept the status quo and who, short of physical violence, work for change where it is needed?

Although we live in this world, we may not always blend too neatly into it. In a sense "this world is not our home." We are just passing through and we want to make a Christian impress on it as we go. We are restless here.

6. *We can understand how God seems to work in the midst of evil and suffering.* We cannot really get at this except through this stance of faith and hope just described. But through this way of looking at things as we read the Bible, as we see the world on the move around us, as we watch the lives of people attempting to do the will of God, as we watch the unfolding of history, we affirm that we do see God at work. And what do we see?

We sense God at work through people, in the human situation, through the operation of his universe to get his will done. He does have purpose. He does have goals. These he does not force upon people. He understands that for them to be effective, this will must be agreed to voluntarily and freely.

God works strongly in situations of evil and suffering as a strength-giver. He doesn't seem often to pick up some burden and carry it away all by himself. But in him we do find strength to cope, to grapple with, to persist, to see things through. In God we find whatsoever it takes to come out with something akin to victory in the battle against evil. "Behold, God is my helper; the Lord is the upholder of my life" (Psalm 54:4).

God seems particularly to have been at work in our world in the face of these basic questions through his Son Jesus Christ. In the New Testament we find Jesus working against evil. We find him teaching a style of life that can bring us through. We find him promising One who will stand by us in all trouble. We find in Jesus' very life itself a story of victory over evil, suffering, and death. Born into a world of travail and tears, misunderstood and opposed, Jesus certainly knew the pain of being human. On a painful cross he met death itself. And then he won a victory in resurrection. Through all of this God was speaking to his lost and erring children. And through his Spirit he continues to minister to us, guide us, give us power.

The issues of evil, suffering, and death will persist for

most people. Here are not answers but ways to stand in light of the issues. Some of these stances will mean more at one time than another in our dynamic, changing, revolving situations. But the man of faith and hope feels that in the face of sorrow and death he has bumped into God and there he has found help.

THINKING THINGS THROUGH

Some Goals

To review how people respond to the fact of evil, suffering, and death when it occurs in the world of a loving, kind God. To consider how to face up to these issues, what stances may be taken in relation to the questions of evil and suffering.

Some Questions to Consider

1. How do you personally answer the question—How can evil, suffering, sorrow, and death exist in the world of a kind, loving powerful God?

2. What does the fact that evil and suffering do seem so strong say to you about God?

3. What kind of life-style in the face of evil and suffering have you developed? How has this changed across the years? How might it yet change as you continue to face this issue?

4. What would you say to a person without faith and hope in God to explain the existence of evil and suffering? What kind of Christian witness can you give him?

5. Which of the stances portrayed in this chapter toward evil and suffering comes closest to your own? Which seems most helpful to you right now? How might these change in their importance for your life?

Some Things to Do

1. Spend several moments in complete silence and meditation. Recall some time when sorrow or evil seemed almost overwhelming in your life. What did the idea of God mean in your life at that time? Think it through for yourself. Share.

2. In a small circle try to explain to one person playing the role of a skeptic or a hopeless victim of evil or suffering, what part God can play in the situation.

7

"Don't We Have Some Mutual Friends?"

Ever notice how in meeting somebody you start groping around to see what mutual friends you have? "Oh, I went to college with a girl who came from Springfield, too." "So you lived in Denver in 1965. Did you know the fellow who operated the Gulf station just off the expressway exit at Littleton?" And so it goes. We seek to establish ties with each other through mutual acquaintances.

On bumping into God, the same sort of thing goes into operation. In fact, our meeting with him probably was brought about through some kind of action by people we know in one way or another. It will be the thesis of this chapter that God does in fact choose frequently to reveal himself to us through people. This knowledge of God can come to us through individual people, deliberately or unconsciously witnessing to the fact of God. It can come to us through well-known Christians or little-known ones. It can come to us through men of today or out of the past. It can come from their words, their songs, their deeds, their very being. It can come out of what these men have done individually in history or out of their united action through the church.

A RELATIVE OF GOD'S

It is altogether appropriate that God should choose to reveal himself so frequently through man. For man is a unique and worthy channel for God's self-revelation. Among all of God's creation, man seems to be uniquely related to God. He is said to be made in the image of God. Two hands and two feet, one nose and one mouth? A head? We don't think so, for God is infinite, not limited in space to certain physical characteristics.

With a personality? There we may be on the trail of something. For if in the ultimate reality or central truth or idea behind the universe we find personal qualities, then man is somehow related. If we find a sense of purpose and consistency, identifiable and unique patterns of behavior and call this God and if we find the same sort of thing in man, then we have established a tie. But don't animals and maybe even insects have some of this, too? Maybe so, and therefore we would have to go beyond the animal to find a unique role in man. There is a clue at this point in the idea that man has a unique purpose and destiny in the world and that he has an openness toward the world and to eternity that lesser animals cannot have. Certainly on the most understandable level, man *appears* to have more understanding of abstract ideas, more appreciation of beauty, more ability to learn from changing experiences than do cats and dogs and butterflies. We would guess that our case might well be proved in scientific testing, but we don't have to rely upon that for our position.

We are taught that man was created in the image of God. "So God created man in his own image, in the image of God he created him" (Genesis 1:27). Like God, man is spirit. The essential quality in him is more than physical, and with that quality he has capacity to have fellowship with God and with other men, even those he has never seen in person. Out of such a fellowship with God in prayer and many kinds of encounters we experience God and we share that experience with others.

Just a word of caution again about how presumptuous man can get in his relationship with God. He can claim too much or too little. He can make such a worm of himself, place himself so far beneath what he feels is the notice of God that he doesn't occupy his rightful place of worth and dignity. No good is served for God or man by such downgrading. At the same time man can perhaps exalt himself too highly. He can place himself at God's right hand or even on the throne of heaven itself. He can presume that what he thinks, what he wants, God therefore automatically thinks and wants also. He can presume that God would be helpless without him. He can presume equality or even superiority. He can merge himself and God with such a result.

The awareness of all the problems with our ecology in recent years has alerted us to another mistaken assumption man can make about himself in God's world. His biblical inheritance tells him that he was created unique and foremost among God's creatures, that he was made to have dominion over all the created world (Genesis 1:26). But there is a major stewardship to that, as we are fast discovering. Being given dominion over the world doesn't free man to mismanage it or to exalt himself in the picture at the expense of all the rest of creation.

Man can too rapidly deplete the natural resources of the earth. He can upset its balance by his destruction of its forests, his diversion and pollution of its waters, his fouling of its air. The balance of nature that supports human life is so delicate that man who sees all the earth set up merely to serve him may destroy it. His nuclear bomb can blow it to bits. He can overpopulate it. He can so retard the photosynthesis process in plants that life processes may slow and even stop.

While traditionally we have seen our universe as a man-centered world under God, we now come to see it under

God as more of a nature-centered world in which man plays a crucial part. In the natural world, man is not merely at the top or at the center but is a vitally important part of the whole. Come scientifically and technically of age, man's responsibilities here are immense.

Such is the man through whom God would reveal himself to our mutual acquaintances.

Now let's look at some of the ways God does work through man as he comes to encounter man.

THE MAN OF HISTORY

God is known through events. Events involve people. It is a moot question whether people create the great forces of history or are shaped by forces beyond their control. No doubt there is a mutual interplay here. Forces, growing out of problems, issues, vast social situations, draw men to them, and the men in turn move them ahead.

Some men are creators, innovators, inventors. They come up with new things, new ways of doing things, new ideas. In the process of bringing together existing ideas and tools and previous creations in new ways, something new is brought into being. So remarkable is this quality, so akin is it to the basic work of God as Creator, that here the action of God is particularly felt. The creative style is one of those characteristics of personality that seems to identify the personal God. It shows up also in his people.

Some men are men of action, doers, forgers of events in history. They make things happen. The result may be judged good or evil. When the result is seen to be good, then it is easy for the observers of that history to understand that here was a man acting for God. The interpretation of good and evil may not always come off that neatly, but the active man who helps accomplish good is one who is most readily understood as an agent of God in Christian society.

Some men exercise power and influence and are understood to be responsible for this under God, who himself is Lord of power and influence. These may be people who rule over other men. They exercise authority and responsibility. Jesus called people "to render unto Caesar the things which are Caesar's" (Matthew 22:21). Paul spoke of people being subject to the governing authorities (Romans 13:1). So we give allegiance to them, at least as far as their rule appears to be in harmony with the will and purposes of God. But here in a special way God may be shown. Here are lives of persons so intimately affected by another that all the great relationship words associated with God, such as love and trust and justice, come into play.

Some men show wisdom and a sense of judgment and perception. Their insight may prove to be so keen in the working out of events of history that the wisdom of God himself seems to be reflected. It goes beyond "common" sense to such a high quality of insight that God appears to be working through men and women of wisdom. Their intuitions and their foresight appear so perceptive and wise that their prophetic quality is recognized. They may seem to speak for God. This can happen at the courthouse, national capitol, or local church when the prophetic quality holds sway. On the other hand, such leaders may also fall desperately short.

So far in this section we seem to be talking about "great" men who have widely influenced the course of history, where across the long centuries we can now look back and make some sense out of it as we see God working. These are public men who achieved fame and whose influence can be individually measured.

THE LITTLE MAN OF FAITH

We don't want to overlook the unknown man or woman, that child or young person who never becomes widely known, who never exercises the kind of creativity, power, wisdom, or perception that wins him fame. But he is no less great in the scheme of things. And in no less an important way may God be revealed through him. There is the farmer who lived a life in tune with his surroundings all his life, at one with God and the creation. There is the woman who worked in an auto parts plant all of her life, never talking much about God but living an upright life of quiet influence. There was the used car salesman who lived a life under heavy competitive and business pressures, who made an ethical slip now and then but who struggled with it, tried to correct it, and found integrity. We could go on and on. It is such individuals that the average man on the street reads and where he either discovers God or misses him.

This is no argument for mediocrity. It is no argument on the other hand for a success-oriented, lift-yourself-by-your-bootstraps religion. God may be revealed through this little man's failures. He may be revealed as the man senses a certain dependency on a source beyond himself for power to live.

IN THE CHURCH

The whole picture isn't painted by individual followers of God. These persons, united in following Jesus Christ to form the body of Christ on earth today, the church, tell together their own story about God.

Let's face it, it may be a pretty sad story sometimes. It may be a picture of hypocrisy as one church-related person after another fails to live up to what he has been taught, to what in God he has experienced. It may be an almost unconscious falling short or outright hypocrisy. It may be sheer failure in the face of heavy opposition and mounting odds. In their divided state, Christians associated with the church may be doing anything but witnessing to the wholeness that is appropriate to God. They may be witnessing to something pretty small, cheap, altogether unworthy of the great God.

For even with its divine quality as the body of Christ, the church is still an institution composed of human beings with shortcomings. Distorted ideas about God can develop. There was the sect, for instance, that argued that God is exactly six feet two inches tall. There is the kind of mentality that gets the church embroiled in arguing about how many angels can swim in a communion cup. All of this may do more to confuse the picture about God than to turn the bright light of understanding upon him.

On the other hand, don't sell the church short. Even in those smallest of situations the church may be showing God's concern for the few, the weak, the persecuted, the limited. Even where distorted ideas appear, a struggle may be under way that ultimately reveals what is for some new truth. Even where hypocrisy shows up, that style of life simply helps set off the more sincere and saintly style of the genuine follower of God. Even where defeat seems to be the byword for the life of the church, genuine triumph shows up, all the more glorious because of the dark days of defeat that surround the gleam of victory.

God seems evident where Christians gather, where the church operates. "Where two or three are gathered together, there am I in the midst," we are promised. A synergism seems to operate here—a case where one and one don't add up to just two. The presence of one Christian with another fosters God-awareness, multiplies skills and talents and muscle. Even Quakers with their stress on one man privately reflecting upon God and reading by his own "inner light," plan for regular meetings where they do this in company with others.

The assembly of Christians can multiply strength. Money is put together. Varied gifts of individual Christians are pooled. Choirs can be formed. There is an electricity in great crowds met together for praise and worship. The presence of one Christian with another multiplies the impact of God on lives. We can do things together that just wouldn't get done separately. No wonder we are called to assemble ourselves together. There is power and direction even in small groups. "If two of you agree on earth about anything they ask, it will be done for them by my Father in heaven. For where two or three are gathered in my name, there I am in the midst of them" (Matthew 18:19-20). No wonder the ideal place part of the time for a Christian is in church, no matter how burdened he may be for the needs of a city slum and how effective he is out there serving God in the world. Of course, he takes the church with him out into the world, too, and this portable church plans its key part in the revelation of God.

PEOPLE UNAWARE

Of course, we can understand God at work, God revealing himself among Christians, among God-aware, Christ-committed people. After all, they are consciously living as God's children. But does God work through other people? Is he revealed through the work of a sincere, committed Buddhist, who is doing a good job of bringing his southeast Asian country into a new and enlightened day? Is God ever at work, perchance, through a committed Chinese Communist politician? Has he ever worked through a general fighting against the United States of America? Has he ever revealed himself through a Mafia chieftan?

The Christian's tendency might well be to think that God surely would not work through such channels. After all, he has us! We do sometimes think of God as working through the founding fathers of America in the establishment of this democracy. And we know that not all of those men were committed Christians.

This section is introduced here to explore the possibility that we sometimes seek to box in God and the ways he works to reveal himself. He can go through any channel. Undoubtedly, making ourselves deliberately available to him is a worthy step that serves God's cause and is a significant act of worship on our part. But God does appear to intervene in history, to work through people in unlimited ways. His ways are past our finding out at this point.

At the end of this chapter we think of many who have brought good news of God—missionaries whose courage and persistence were so great that good news about God was taken to faraway shores, into new cities. We could turn to great men of the pulpit who have proclaimed good news with unusual power and persuasiveness. Probably it would be more in the spirit of Christ in all this for us to keep turning, again and again, to the men and women, boys and girls who live out rather ordinary lives that seem to point toward God. Maybe words have been involved now and then, but more often deeds and just being have been the indicators.

THINKING THINGS THROUGH

Some Goals

To understand that God chooses to reveal himself through people—persons acting in history, both well-known and little known, persons in the church, persons who have written the Bible under his inspiration, persons even unaware of what they were doing to reveal God's ways.

To consider who man is and how God works through him.

To share in the church's life and work as a channel for doing God's work and revealing him to this generation.

Some Questions to Consider

Why do you think God has chosen to reveal himself to the world so much through people? What are the strengths and

95

problems for revelation going through such a channel?

How can you tell when God is working in history?

What special ways and what advantages do you see for God to work through little-known, everyday people compared with famous people?

What are the advantages and disadvantages for God working through a whole group of people, as in the church?

Do you agree or disagree that God works sometimes through people who are not religious, who even may be his enemies?

Some Things to Do

Recall or look up some events in history at random. Choose two or three. Then describe how God might have been at work here.

Think of people who have been influential in your life. How was God working through them?

Consider how God might speak through you in your community. Plan a witness or service project to implement that.

8

"I Just Can't Believe It"

"Now if I ever actually bump into God on the street, maybe I could believe in him," said one young person. "As it is, I never have seen him or met anybody I believed had seen him. He never spoke to me in any kind of voice you could put on a tape recorder."

Chances are, even if this young man were to bump into Somebody called God, he'd still have his troubles. God could be standing there with a sandwich board on him proclaiming that this is indeed God. The fact could be attested to on an impressive gold-sealed certificate from Price Waterhouse or the Chase Manhattan Bank, and he still couldn't believe. God could be standing there working a miracle with one hand and healing a child with the other. Seraphim could be fluttering around his feet and a flashing, neon-lit halo could be lighting up his head. And that still wouldn't make our young skeptic believe.

FACE UP TO THE DIFFICULTIES OF BELIEVING

Belief is not easy to come by in our day. In the first place, the person may not want to believe, and then the God-advocate has an almost impossible job. In the second place the person may not care too much about believing. It may just not be important to him. He can take it or leave it—mostly leave it—while he gives his attention somewhere else. Or the person may deeply, honestly want to believe, but he keeps running into roadblocks that shut off his faith. Often our views are mixed like the father of the boy with convulsions brought to Jesus: "I believe; help my unbelief" (Mark 9:24).

Let's face it: belief often comes most easily to the simple-minded, uncomplex person. And almost everything works against our being simple-minded and uncomplex these days. The very education that sets us free from superstition and ignorance may bring us such an inquiring style of thinking, so much skepticism, that we find it hard to make a simple, all-out commitment or to put our faith in any one thing. The spirit of skepticism is strong in the land, and it is catching. No one wants to look like any more of a babe-in-the-woods than he has to in a grown man's world where doubting is the style.

Our forebears in a less complicated day understood little about the workings of their world and just had to put their trust in more things. In the big areas of mystery about why nature acted the way it did, God was conveniently brought in to fill the gap. With those things man could do very little about, he had to do more leaning on something. And where you have to lean with a bit of uncertainty, there you just have to develop some trust. But through it all has come the steady march of technology. Science has pushed back the frontiers. The surface of the moon isn't so much of a mystery any more. The causes and cures of countless diseases have been found. The technological age breaks up old patterns of belief, and new patterns have not taken their place for many persons in the midst of our late twentieth-century scientific era.

The availability of mountains of information has its effect on the patterns of belief. We are flooded by information, as rapidly as computers can print out their vast stores of data. Radio and television news and information programs burst in on us from every side with instantaneous coverage of events around the world. Magazines and newspapers feed the public hunger for still more data. We get in the habit of living with mountains of information. Rumor, hearsay, casual opinion, may not be enough. We may not even trust our own experience in the face of the information explosion. A person oriented to living by data is not necessarily ready to live by the old patterns of belief.

We have lived through an era that has been shattering to a faith of optimism. This century has been clouded constantly by giant wars and rumors of such wars. Old values have sometimes been caught short in meeting the tests of new crises. Totalitarian forces have made sneak attacks. Colossal bombs have been dropped. Great powers, in the name of right, have subjected small nations to long-drawn-out wars not of their own making. East has been aligned against West. Leaders have been martyred. The times have been sick. On a more personal level many youth have found sham in the middle-class lives of their parents, and adults have been shocked at the rebellion of their children. Family life has been severely tried. It is the day of the false front and the big boast. Crime multiplies. Not exactly a time to foster trust, belief, or faith!

And yet through it all faith has survived. The forms of that faith have sometimes been changed. Religious faith has had its ups and downs across the last twenty years, but faith keeps struggling along.

Come to think of it, faith is still a necessity in life. You have to put your faith in something just to get by. You trust the driver in the approaching lane of traffic to stay there—and most of the time he does. You trust the dairy to bottle reasonably pure milk without putting poison into it—and, except for those occasional traces of pollution and radioactive substances we hear about, we can trust the product. Not to have any trust would soon drive us all into a state of paranoia that would turn the world into one vast mental institution.

But the realm of religion faces a world that has notably lost faith in spiritual matters. What approach shall be taken by the person who now doubts or the person seeking to help others come to faith in God?

You can turn pretty fatalistic about it for one thing. You can say that a person either is going to believe or he isn't and let it go at that. Such an attitude has its points, but it is not going to satisfy the God-believer, who as a part of his belief just must share it. Such a person is going to live out his faith. He is going to talk about it at every opportunity. The response may or may not come, but he is going to share. And, too, history shows that such sharing does, despite everything, grab people. A certain number of persons will catch a faith in just that way.

You can get busy and try to push people into faith as another response to the dilemma. Arm twisting. Holding out promise of reward. Issuing warnings of punishment. But increasingly with a more sophisticated kind of people all around us this hasn't been working. We get some clues from current ideas about education as to why this doesn't really work too well any more and as to what directions we can move in.

Repeated testing and widespread observation show that learning (and faith is a kind of learning) has to be done by the learner himself. Nobody else, not even his would-be teacher, can do it for him. Outside forces by themselves will not cause him to learn unless he decides within himself that he needs to learn this and that it will be of benefit to him. Things from outside may stimulate him properly or improperly. Some of these forces may actually inhibit him in the long run and turn him away. Holding up ideas of special rewards or fears of certain reprisals won't in themselves cause him to learn (to have faith, in this case).

In fact under such stimuli some individuals find that the harder they try, the worse things get. It's like telling yourself as you lie restlessly in bed at two in the morning, "You just must go to sleep; you have a hard day tomorrow." The more you tell yourself that under pressure the harder it is to sleep. In the same way, the more desperately you tell yourself, "I must have faith," the harder it may be for you to achieve it.

You can take either positive or negative attitudes toward doubt as you quest for faith in yourself or for others. One attitude fears doubt. It would wish it away, not admit that it should ever be permitted to be around, oppose it on every turn. And there is a reasonableness to this. You would think, just by looking at doubt, that obviously here is an enemy of the faith that must be vanquished. Poor old doubting Thomas has always been under a cloud with faithful Christians. Just build up your faith, we're told, and send old Doubt running with his tail between his legs. And good riddance!

I'm not too friendly with Doubt myself. He's a troublesome fellow who leaves you feeling pretty empty when he gives you a good battle. He may keep God from working (as in Matthew 13:58). But we have to assume one thing: Doubt is around and is pretty strong these days. He isn't really going to run off soon. The more we try to attack him head on the more, like worrying about a sleepless night, he's going to keep sticking his nose into our business. So perhaps there is some accepting we can do here. Take modern man in the condition where he is—and that situation is full of doubt.

Next look on the better side of doubt and see how useful that can be. For one thing doubt is not absolute rejection of the faith. That's in its favor. Doubt allows a person to be open toward the truth we want him to come to. In fact, doubt may be the prodding agent that eventually spurs a person into new insights and greater understanding. Doubt may help the person review and cast off some old misconceptions he has had. Doubt allows a person to apply his emotions to a situation where perhaps before he had only an intellectual stance.

Or, on the other hand, doubt may allow a person to bring to bear his intellect on a situation where before only his emotions held sway. Doubt is an agent that allows a person to test things out. A firm Christian is likely to believe that the faith he represents can stand any of this testing. So doubt can become the pathway to greater faith. Actually, the sickness of a lot of people these days is that they don't even bother to doubt. They are too preoccupied with lesser things, or they are putting their faith or their doubts on the wrong things.

Another approach we can take as we face the issue of people without faith is not to expect the whole thing to be handled at once. We may expect that sometimes, with the suddenness of a conversion, a person will move from unfaith to faith. This does happen. At the same time it may be, in fact, a little dangerous when that does seem to take place. The old doubts may only have been buried temporarily in the light of a new affection, but they will come creeping out later on.

Some issues just are going to keep on pestering us. For most people who think a lot the problems of evil and suffering just hardly ever get completely wrapped up to stay. They keep coming around. You might just settle back in a chair and conclude that there is a mystery here, that the Christian faith is full of mysteries that in this life we are never going to understand. We can kick against the pricks and keep struggling in a defeated way with such issues. Or we can allow faith to take over, riding with its swells and troughs and accepting strength from God to meet the issues.

Another approach is to try to persuade the person into faith, argue with him if necessary, using whatever logic or philosophy we can muster. We are surveying some of these arguments for God elsewhere. You can argue back from effect to cause; there has to be an intelligent first cause for the orderly world we live in. You can argue that if it is possible for man to conceive of a great God, then he would have to be possible in our system. And so on. But the record does not really show that many have been won to a faith in God through such a channel. Their faith has come in other ways.

There is room here for what is sometimes called "suspended judgment." Not everything has to be completely and nicely wrapped up at once. Life is too complicated for that. The mysteries of the universe and the ways of God are too complex for us to fit them into neat little boxes. By accepting the idea of suspended judgment, we tackle only a few things at a time, being content to leave the rest in suspended judgment until we get around to them later. This is an agonizing state for some people who just must have all the answers, but it is a style that fits into the way God works.

Christ taught his disciples some things, but in their brief time together Jesus knew he couldn't teach them everything and they couldn't fully grasp even all that he did bring to them. So he promised them the Holy Spirit who would come to add light later to what he had taught, who would strengthen them and help them as they matured in the faith. There is plenty of evidence—from Peter's denial to other shallow insights expressed by Jesus' followers—that they didn't grasp everything at once. They had to live by suspended judgment and limited insights while they matured in the faith.

ON TO FAITH

Relax. Strange advice? Isn't it better to struggle, to strain, to try hard for faith? Maybe so, but that's not quite what is meant here. Sometimes the straining after faith itself is the hangup. This approach is related to the willingness to do a couple of things that can in the long run build faith. One is the willingness to suspend judgment we have discussed. We don't need to have final and complete answers right here and right now. The second is some willingness to trust the blanks in our knowledge, in fact to trust the situation we're in with the confidence that it can be worked out.

My coaching friends tell me that one thing they go after in preparing athletes for a big game is to get them to relax. The athlete, it appears, performs at his best when he is not under tensions that tighten him up. "Hang loose!" the coaches say. How does this fit into being "up" for the big game? The two are not opposites that don't fit together. One may be at his best if he is both relaxed and confident as well as alert and on his toes to make the most of the situations the game will bring to him. A similar approach would seem to prepare the way for faith. Relax in God or in whatever state you find yourself, but also be alert, open, and ready to receive the insights that come to you.

We are especially well advised not to tighten up in the face of doubt or to feel estranged from God and from Christians should doubt seem to have closed a door to them. Doubt instead, as we have already discussed, can be a useful tool in reaching new levels of faith.

Staying free from being uptight about matters of faith can also give us perspective and allow us to be open to new insights. Being uptight can hang us up on the least crucial matters of faith.

Be Informed. Far from being an enemy of faith, education is a gateway to new dimensions of trusting commitment. It is true that for some people a little knowledge is a dangerous thing. A little knowledge is like a small camp-fire in the forest. We huddle by it, as it lights up a tiny area closely surrounded by the darkness. As we add wood to the fire and it leaps higher and higher, a wider area is illuminated. No longer does the dark press in so closely. Now the night is pushed farther away. But the dark areas are still there, actually looking bigger and bigger. The more we know, the more areas calling for the investigation of our faith are opened up.

Study will open doors to new areas where faith is called for. Study can undergird faith. It provides data for our faith, something to think about, new ideas to challenge and call forth our faith.

A whole range of areas calls us to study for the broad information we need. Centrally, this speaks of the Bible and those study tools that help us understand the Bible. It may mean reading history, philosophy, and theology at appropriate levels of our understanding.

Open-eyed Expectancy. Ever notice how much more you get out of something after you have looked forward to it for a while? Long-dreamed-of pleasures seem to mean considerably more than what comes up on the spur of the moment or accidentally. Faith in God appears to be on the same order. If it is just handed to us on a silver platter, it doesn't mean so much as when we have to work for it, build it with our own sweat and muscle. This is the trouble with faith that really belongs to parents or to some influential friend but which we haven't worked out for ourselves. This is the trouble with a churchly creed we repeat without building into our own lives. There's certainly nothing wrong with a faith being handed to us at home, in a church service, or a church school class. Trouble comes only if we do not receive it with a sense of open-eyed expectancy and build it deliberately into our lives.

Expectancy says that we do live in hope of something good coming our way. It says we have confidence that insights and new understanding will appear, that these will have something of value to say to our lives. There are overtones of expectancy, touches of youthful enthusiasm for what is about to appear.

Notice that this is *open-eyed* expectancy. It is not naive, blindly accepting just any idea that comes on the scene. It does not fail to discriminate, to weigh against all else that we could believe. It does not accept blindly anything that comes without first placing it in the whole picture of faith that we have developed till now. It is not accepted unless it ties in with all the information we have been accumulating and the wisdom that we already possess. It is the questioning expectancy of one like Nicodemus who kept coming to Jesus with his queries (John 3:1; 7:50).

All of this is saying that it pays to live an open style of life, being sensitive to and ready for insights, hungry for what can round out our life view and make us wiser, more dedicated, more effective persons.

The Obedient Style of Life. The discipline of obedience is not a strong or popular approach to living for many people these days. We tend to place currently a strong emphasis on individual freedom. Yet there is still room and high value in the obedient, serving, style of life that is marked by discipline under Christ's law of love. This obedience, this discipline lay a foundation for faith even when life situations are not fully understood. While the Bible places great stress on the life of faith, it also makes room for works. Doing the truth can lead to a firmer grasp of it.

Relate to a Person. It is easier to believe in someone you know personally than someone known only through the pages of a newspaper or a history book. You have no doubts about the existence of a brother you see every day. This is the key to faith. Faith cannot be built on mere knowledge *about* a God off somewhere or a person named Jesus Christ described in the pages of a black-covered book.

It is between persons that the elements of faith come to full flower rather than in the philosopher's ivory tower or in the scholar's library.

This is to say that faith can be built out of human relations with other people, where ideals of trust, hope, faith, love, are put into practice. Since you cannot control another human being, especially all of his inner feelings and desires, any such relationship must be built on trust. Any interchange between you is best handled as an act of love. Any permanent relationship between you is best based on some commitment of friendship and love to each other.

This carries over into the dimensions of faith in God. For many people this comes most graphically and with most meaning as we bring ourselves into a personal relationship with Christ. It is person to person. We are persons with a degree of freedom to make or withhold commitment, feelings of loyalty, a desire to understand, a desire to give ourselves, a capacity for intimacy, a need to show and receive love. Christ puts the face and the personality into our understanding of God and can be the basis of our relationship of faith. "He who has seen me has seen the Father" (John 14:9).

In this tie with Jesus Christ we give ourselves to him through an act of commitment. In him we find forgiveness. Through him we have our lives turned around. In such a very personal relationship we find the basis for faith in God. This is apart from any theoretical or merely philosophical search for faith. Through a personal tie, we find the relationship on which faith develops. Doubt may not be defeated. Distrust may arise. Faith may be challenged, but through it all the personal relationship, on which a permanent and abiding faith can be built, is there.

THINKING THINGS THROUGH

Some Goals

To consider how faith develops in people and to take steps that encourage personal growth in trusting acceptance of God.

To discuss the role of doubt as a means of strengthening faith.

To examine the condition of modern man in a day of technology and knowledge explosions that can either undermine or strengthen the life of faith.

Some Questions to Consider

Why is it that some people find it hard to believe in God while others find it easy?

How can science and the knowledge explosion hinder faith? help it?

What does doubt do for you in building up or tearing down faith?

What steps toward developing a stronger faith would you suggest?

Some Things to Do

Get with other people and role play one person being torn with doubts about God and another trying to help him strengthen his faith.

Work on a definition of "Christian doubt." What is doubt that is Christian? What is doubt that is unchristian?

Make a private list of things that you most surely believe. Make a private list of matters related to the Christian faith that you feel uncertain about. In this last list, decide on which items you can suspend judgment for a while and which you would like to work on in order to arrive at a more satisfying stand.

Make a study of references to the apostle Thomas and his doubting (Matthew 10:3; Mark 3:18; Luke 6:15; Acts 1:13; John 11:16; 20:24-27; 21:2). Why would Jesus have called such a man? What does he contribute to us?

9

"Say, Could You Spare a Quarter?"

The pain is unbearable. "Oh, help me, God."

The night moves toward dawn, and still Jackie hasn't returned. "Bring her home safely, Lord."

It is a bloody battle. The sniper fire comes close. "Help me get through this, God."

The new job would mean everything in the world. Plenty of money. Opportunity for advancement. Prestige. "Help me get it, Lord."

According to a recent poll across America, more people offer prayers like this than say they actually believe in the existence of God. When we get into a jam, when we want something extraordinarily, when the pain gets strong enough, we pray—whether or not we believe in God.

Need drives people to God. When things get out of their own control, when they feel the need of strength from beyond themselves, when they don't have the resources or know where else to find them, in desperation they may turn to God. Vernard Eller has pointed out that if man doesn't need God, then his existence is beside the point. Limiting as such an approach to God may appear, the fact remains that many, many people bump into God only when driven to him out of desperation.

And then they come to him like beggars, asking for his dimes and quarters to meet their problems. They come to him, maybe only half believing in him, maybe not even really believing in him at all but willing in their desperation to play any chance that maybe, just maybe through some magic there is some Ultimate Reality out there with the power to help them in their plight.

WE COME TO GOD, ASKING

Believing or not, we *ask* God. Too bad that for so many of us this is one of the few bridges with God that exists. But it is there, born not just of desperation or wild hope but often of a sound trust in a God one loves. And when we come asking—if we take time to think at all—some questions occur to us.

1. *When you ask God for something, does it make any difference who you are?* It would be only normal to assume that faithful old Aunt Jenny, who has lived as a devoted Christian all her life, is more likely to be heard than just a man who has scarcely bothered to doff his cap to the idea of God in forty years. It would be only normal to assume that God would give special attention to his favorite people. And it would be reasonable to assume that his favorite people are those in the church, those who have obeyed his laws, who have long sought to do his will. It is this kind of expectation that led, no doubt, to the system of seeking to enlist special saints on your side if you pray in the style of many Roman Catholics. It should be a help to have somebody intercede for you. It is the same expectation which sends someone else to his pastor or to the elders of the church or to a person in whose faith you have special confidence. Get this person on your side. Get this person praying for you. And this does seem to help.

There is considerable evidence, however, that God doesn't play favorites when it comes to hearing. In fact, there seems to be some indication that the person with the biggest need, the one coming out of the greatest desperation and earnestness is the one who is most likely to be heard. At the same time, the man of faith assumes that whoever calls on God with sincerity is going to be heard. The biblical phrases pile up: "Come to me, all who labor and are heavy laden" (Matthew 11:28), "Let him who is thirsty come, let him who desires take the water of life without price" (Revelation 22:17).

2. *Does the way we pray, the form of our approach to God make any difference?* This question is akin to the first one. God reads the heart and when he finds there sincerity, earnestness, real need, he is going to listen. Not that there aren't some approaches that may be more helpful to some of us than other ways of praying. One person finds that if he comes pouring out his heart in real thankfulness to God, the prayer communication begins to work. Another person comes expressing his joy and wonder in the Lord, and enters into communion with God. Still another kind of person is helped if the situation is one of high worship, surrounded by others at worship, by great gothic windows, singing choirs, exalted music. Another person may be helped by the simplest, most direct kind of word he can utter. Still others may have to clear things up between themselves and others and God by confessing their wrongdoings, their own smallness, and God's greatness.

Jesus offered us a sample prayer in Matthew 6 and Luke 11. It is a great prayer which bears repeating. Part of its greatness is not in any magic prayer formula we may find in it, but in the fact that it combines a number of these elements just surveyed, any one of which may be what best opens the door of communication with God for us.

3. *Does chance make any difference when we pray?* The question is a fair one because people, in their own experience and in hearing the prayers of others, figure

that some prayers have been answered and others have not been. They see two people of apparently equal need and piety both pray about similar problems. One seems to find a remedy and the other seems not to. Some prayers appear to be answered immediately, others only gradually, and still others to outward appearance not at all.

We try to explain these differences in various ways. Some people would say that there must be a hidden difference in the amount of faith these two had, and that the person with the greater faith had the more immediate answer. Others would say that there must be some hidden flaw or barrier in the life of the person whose prayer was not answered. Others would look to God himself in this and figure that he is answering according to his own purposes, that his replies fit in with his long-range purposes which we do not fully understand. They would say that out of his greater perspective on what is good for us, God is dealing with each according to his need. But since we don't know the whole picture, his responses don't always make full sense to us. Some might say that God rewards one person and punishes another by the way he answers.

As we see elsewhere in our consideration of who God is and how he relates himself to us and our needs, there is much we don't understand about God and the way he works in our lives. The man of faith accepts God's answers, whether that answer is a yes, a no, a maybe, or a later. Not that such a person becomes a blindly accepting, less-than-human blotter, automatically soaking up whatever it is he feels God hands out. He just has to accept some mystery here, as long as he figures that God is fair and just and lovingly sensitive. And he needs some openness toward the grace of God. This last we soon shall discuss more fully.

4. *Do we actually change God's mind in prayer?* Some people ask: Who are we to change God's mind? He is sup-

posed to be all-wise, all-powerful, constantly loving, gracious. If he knows so much and is so concerned about us, why do we have to pray? When the old motto said, "Prayer changes things," was that talking about God's mind, his will, and his intentions? Or was it saying that prayer in reality changes us, brings us more in tune with God's will?

If it is not God's mind or his way of doing anything that is changed in prayer, why do we offer prayers asking him to do something for us? Why do we ask him for healing and hope and other help? Why don't we just limit our prayers, as some people would have us do, to those words where we seek to know God's will, commit ourselves to that, express our love for God, offer our praise to him, seek to be guided by him, ask his forgiveness. After all, those are enough items to fill up our prayer life from now on.

Let's propose, in the first place, that most of our prayer life ought to be the kind of two-way communication that will enable us to get in tune with God along the lines just mentioned. Let's agree to give higher priority in this direction than in asking God for things where it might be presumed that we are asking God to change his mind.

Then at the same time, let's propose that it is in God's provision that we really let him know how we feel about things and that he does hear and respond to us. That response can well allow for God to change his way of working or to take direct action on our behalf where he had not been expecting to. This is not forcing some complete change of course in God's ways. It is part of a mutual response back and forth between God and man, as he adjusts to our humanness and our free will and as we adjust to his sovereignty. Such a give-and-take can well fit into the highest kind of fellowship between God and his creation.

TOWARD A WIDER VIEW OF PRAYER

Much of what we have been discussing so far has been centered on prayer as asking. Prayer is certainly that and worthily so, but we have been implying that it is other things as well. The way we see prayer and our understanding of it is closely related to the way we have experienced God and have sensed his relationship to us.

If we see God high and lifted up, looking down on the earth and its daily routines from a vast distance, if we see him as some great ruler on a throne, prayer is going to be a different sort of thing than if we see God as part of our very own being, closer than breath itself and pervading all that we do.

In the first instance, prayer becomes an exalted act where great distance is felt between the humble person at prayer and the majestic object of his prayers. Here great care in wording the prayer would be taken and only the most proper of forms would be used. In the later instance, if God is indeed within one and is closer than breathing, then prayer need hardly be a conscious act at all. Each thought, each action can be a kind of prayer.

Since we are affirming on faith in this book that God is both that high and exalted One and that one who is as close as breathing, then a whole range of ways of relating with him through prayer seems appropriate.

Prayer, understood as a two-way communication between God and man expressed in words, thoughts, deeds, and life-style, becomes one of the chief ways we know and relate to God. Without trying to be comprehensive, let's look at some of the functions we exercise in prayer to consider how these may relate us more closely with God.

Listening. We were thinking of prayer earlier as asking. But also important in all our relationships—with other people as well as with God—is this idea of listening. This means more than turning up the hearing aid or being silent.

It means more than taking accurate notes from a lecturer. It involves openness toward the one we would listen to, an expectation that there is something here to learn, something worth remembering.

Perhaps you have noticed that you receive more from a speaker when you listen to him with expectancy rather than a sense of duty, dread, or boredom. It involves sensitivity to the one we listen to. What is he saying between the lines? What do we know from his background and previous experiences that help explain his whole being to us as a framework for the words? It means hearing with the expectation of active response to what is being said, not just a passive soaking up of information.

Part of this response may be dialogue with the speaker on the basis not of thinking what you are going to say while the other person is speaking, but really hearing him and then responding precisely to that. Listening, really listening, involves a certain perspective of knowledge and understanding in the whole area under discussion; we don't come to good listening as a perfect blank or out of ignorance. There is a certain humility in listening—the sense of realizing that we don't already know it all and that we need to know more from this person now communicating with us. A most important part of prayer life is listening. In this way we draw upon God's wisdom, his guidance, sense his feelings, know something of his will.

Thanksgiving, Adoration, Praise. "My soul magnifies the Lord, and my spirit rejoices in God my Savior, for he has regarded the low estate of his handmaiden" (Luke 1:46-48). For many people, the channels to God are best opened up when they come to him expressing their gratitude, voicing their feelings toward him in praise and adoration. These are common enough words, but they are still slightly strange in the everday culture in which we live. We say, "Thank you," frequently but often as a matter of routine courtesy without any real sense of gratitude. It is simply a way of lubricating the routine relationships of the day and making the way of life smoother.

The mood of the day often tends to be more of cynicism and skepticism about people rather than any real sense of praise and gratitude for the good in them that does show up in our fast-moving and sleek society. The mood of the day is toward self-reliance or at least reliance on forces over which we have some control. All of this works against the moods reflected in thanksgiving, adoration, and praise —especially when it comes to this unseen factor that some of us call God.

Yet, the man of faith who approaches God in prayer does himself and those around him good and opens up the channels to God by these expressions of grateful relationship. He puts himself in proper relationship to God—who is the giver while we are the receiver, who is the great and glorified one while we are the limited creation. This helps us put things in perspective. It does us good to express praise and thanksgiving to others and is a vehicle for our love and devoted service to ride upon. Ever notice how you feel toward someone after you have expressed genuine thanks and praise toward him. You feel somehow more open and more closely tied to him. You have an investment in him now. These are key words in the wider meanings of prayer.

Confession. Guilt is a pervading illness in our society. Psychiatrists seem to help a number of people achieve new stability in their lives by hearing them pour out their inner feelings of guilt. While Protestants may not agree with all the implications of the Roman Catholic confessional, the human therapeutic value of such acts, with one human being telling another about his transgressions, cannot be denied. Sometimes Christians, feeling that their whole way of life must be addressed to the right, build up great burdens of guilt as they fall short of goals, as they make mistakes, as the errors of their lives creep back into the picture. God hears our heartfelt repentance.

So confession of wrongdoing, poor attitudes, shortcomings can perform wonders in opening up the channels of communication in prayer. The act of confession with the accompanying sense of God's forgiveness is a keynote in good mental health alone. What it does in one's basic relationship with God and other people under Christ goes immeasurably beyond even that important life factor. We do find God forgiving, even as the psalmist did: "For thou, O Lord, art good and forgiving, abounding in steadfast love to all who call on thee" (Psalm 86:5).

Setting for Prayer. Closets for prayer, kneeling benches, altars, bedsides—these all come to mind as we consider where prayer may best take place. These speak of special "holy places" and designated areas for prayer. Such may help. Going to church to pray, entering a special prayer chapel may be of some assistance. Certainly listening to inspiring music, reading devotional passages in the Bible, reading devotional magazines, engaging in periods of quiet meditation, may help set the stage for prayer. Such have proved to be valuable aids across the years. They are fine as long as the settings do not become substitutes for real prayer itself or such dull routine that the doors of communication are closed.

For some people, at least, variety in situations and moods are an aid to vital prayer. A changing rhythm for prayer life in withdrawn settings and out in the streets, in church, and home and neighborhood, kneeling with eyes shut and standing with eyes open to the needs of the world, at high noon or at dawn or at three A.M., alone, with others—these can help keep up a rich and varied pattern in prayer life.

Praying alone at some frequent points would seem to

be an essential within the full range of prayer life. When the communication responsibility rests more directly on the person, the chances for concentration are enhanced. He can feel directly the two-way, person-to-Person intercommunion.

But prayer is not always a one-to-One matter, although that is how many people feel about it even in church as they listen to the public, pastoral prayer. It can take on rich group aspects. Praying together, in unison with others, in their presence, with focus on the same thoughts, seems greatly to strengthen the effectiveness of communication. One-plus-one in prayer equals more than two. Add in still others agreeing together in prayer and the total results are multiplied, so it seems in experience.

Spirit of Prayer. Nor is prayer a matter of words alone passing back and forth between God and man. It may be a song that is sung, a sigh that is uttered, a hand clasped, a knee bent, a look of sympathy and compassion, a strong muscle flexed in service. It may be a life lived in the spirit of prayer.

This is the fundamental style of life that it would seem God and man might best agree upon as a basis for their relationship to one another. Since prayer doesn't have to be put in words (though that should often happen) and since prayer doesn't have to take place in a certain sacred spot (though places of prayer are helpful), the whole of a life attuned to God can be lived in a spirit of prayer. This makes giving a cup of cold water to a thirsty one an act of prayer. It can make tightening a bolt on an assembly line an act of prayer. It can make the preparation of the evening meal an act of prayer.

The whole, God-conscious style of life can be a life of prayer. Then it really isn't a matter of "bumping" into God casually, perhaps accidentally, any more. Now meeting God everywhere and deliberately is the expected thing. Engaging in life with him is the style.

THINKING THINGS THROUGH

Some Goals

To understand prayer as a basic way of relating oneself to God.

To explore the meaning of prayer as two-way communication with God, including asking, listening, offering thanksgiving and praise, confession. To understand how it involves a person in a whole way of life.

To deal with some of the hindrances that block meaningful prayer.

Some Questions to Consider

1. How do you feel—does it make a difference to God who you are when you come praying? Does the form of our prayer really make much difference? Do we really change God's mind when we pray? Do we change ourselves?

2. What does listening in prayer really mean to you? What all is involved?

3. What kind of setting best helps you concentrate in prayer?

4. Has the style of your prayer life changed any in recent years? Have you grown in some particular way in your experience of prayer?

Some Things to Do

1. Try some new things in prayer to see if this adds growth and freshness to your prayer life. Try praying on a city street with your eyes open. Try praying in a circle of fellow Christians for each one with your eyes open. Try writing a prayer letter to God, making the very act of writing it out a prayer. Think about making some daily routine of yours deliberately into a prayer, considering what all is involved in your doing that.

2. Interview several people about their prayer life. When and how do they pray? What have been their experiences in receiving answers?

3. Read prayers in the Bible and consider what the people in those prayers learned about God through the experience. You might write down some of these learnings. You can read Abraham's prayer beginning in Genesis 18:23; Jacob's in Genesis 32:24; Solomon's in 1 Kings 3:6; Ezra's in Ezra 9:6; Habakkuk's in Habakkuk 3:1; the Lord's prayer in Matthew 6:9; Christ's intercessory prayer in John 17.

10

"My Lord and My God"

You walk up to this acquaintance on the corner. You smile and say, "How do you do, sir. You are my lord and my God."

Not very likely. Not if you have all your wits about you. Nor would you do this very often. We just don't commit ourselves that way.

OTHER "GODS"

On second thought, maybe we commit ourselves too glibly, to too many different things. We may say to keeping our house clean: "You are my god." And so a woman spends her days scrubbing and polishing an already immaculate home. She may put that above the comfort and convenience of her family. She may put it above loving her husband. She may put it above service to her community and above faithful worship at church.

We may say to the dollar, shrinking though it does: "You are my god." And so earning the buck, working one job, two jobs, three jobs to earn money, may take the place of family living, of Christian service, of caring for one's body, mind, and spirit. The power, influence, and gadgets that money can buy may occupy the center of the stage as devotion to this lord takes priority.

We may, in fact, say to another person, "You are my lord and my master, my god." With varying shades of difference, this may be a daughter, a husband, a friend, a hero, a political leader. Granting the worth of patriotism and loyalty to one's country, not even the most excellent president can demand a loyalty that rightfully belongs to God. Certainly there is little room in this category for a sports hero or a movie star, or even a great social or religious leader, if that loyalty is to surpass a commitment to the Highest of all.

We may even say to good works, "You are my god." In such acts the person is trying to work out his salvation by good deeds. He may devote his whole life to a do-good vocation, or spend many hours each week trying to help people. But if he makes of this service his lord and god he has missed the point. The result is that his service may be shallow, without long-range point and meaning. The people he seeks to help may only feel patronized or used to feed the ego of the would-be servant. The acts of helpfulness themselves may not be accompanied by a rich spirit of love and devotion.

We may say to what we *think* is God, "My Lord and my God," but really have hold of the wrong thing. Because if we have a badly shrunken, lopsided, or mistaken view of God, when we give our loyalty to him, we may just be fooling ourselves, misleading ourselves and perhaps others. This is giving loyalty to the too-small God J. B. Phillips wrote about several years ago. That too-small God is still among us, at least in the minds of people.

This is the kindly "man upstairs" God who is simply a good neighbor to you and who does little beyond that. This is the errand-boy God who is at your bidding to do little things for your convenience. This is the stern grandfather God. This is the God who is so far away or so near at hand he really doesn't fill out the whole picture of God that is needed in our world of today. This is the patriotic American or Canadian God, who is always on the side of our country, whether it be right or wrong. Such are concepts of God that are really too small to command and deserve our highest loyalty. All in all, we run various risks with the commandment, "You shall have no other Gods before me" (Exodus 20:3).

WHAT WE HAVE TO GIVE

My affirmation in this book is that the great and glorious, close and loving God is here and calls us to commit ourselves to him in all his fullness. My affirmation also is that we are fully capable of giving him that commitment, that it means much to him and to us. This is a commitment that means something because we are made to be free persons with the power to choose. Certainly it is true that we are hemmed in by our background, our heritage, the place where we live in the world, the kind of training we have received. But it remains that we were created free and to be free. We can get over the personal hangups that inhibit us and shut us in. We can get past the chains that would bind us to all the customs and minor loyalties that would keep us from this supreme commitment.

This commitment also means a great deal because God has created us to be human beings. To call ourselves human is really to say something important. While there are limitations in our status as created beings—which we need to learn to live with—the idea of being human speaks more of possibilities than of limitations. Great are the talents, the energies, the understandings, the capacities, the love, that we can offer to God and share with other people because we are human. It is a part of our commitment to God that we are helped thereby to be free and to be more fully human.

Adding further significance to this commitment is the way it can put us in tune with God's great creative powers. Adding to our own creativeness we can build much that will glorify God, serve man, and further God's world. The great symphony, the important painting, the skillful, humble act of service—these are but samples of how our creativity and God's can come together in the act of commitment for the benefit of all.

This commitment is made in light of the fact that we are created in the image of God and, despite our sins and weaknesses, are related to him to start with. God is spirit, God is personal. We also are spirit and personal. Through conscious dedication, these are brought together, put in harmony. Man himself feels the result of this as for the first time, with God fitting harmoniously into his life, he becomes whole. His high purposes are brought into right priority. He is in tune with things. He becomes complete.

WHAT GOES INTO OUR CONFESSION?

The words of our confession to God, "You are my Lord and my God," are meant to be more than words. They involve our whole beings. For the sake of analysis, let's look at some of the aspects of what this confession of faith really means.

First of all, it isn't just something we do. God is involved, and we come to him in commitment out of response to what he has done. He has been trying to get through to us. He has been trying to reveal himself to us in many ways. He sent his son Jesus to earth to work out our salvation for us, and it was at great cost. God has showed his great forgiving love for us.

Now we are making this commitment as a response, with great feeling. We really mean it and sense it to the depths of our hearts. It is, in significant part, an emotional matter. All of our sense of love and devotion, admiration and praise, pour into it. It is in no way casual, held back by reservations.

At the same time it is not only emotional. That would not be enough. We make the commitment with all our wits about us. We have thought it through. It is an intellectually respectable thing that we do. With our best thinking and all our mind we believe in what we are doing. We have met God and we know it is best that we give ourselves to him.

This act of giving ourselves comes also from the will and the muscle. We have decided here. Our blood pressure has risen in the process of carrying out this act of the will. Our muscles are tied in with it. We are acting purposefully, not just going through mental and emotional gymnastics. The act of making this choice is of one piece with the actions that will follow and grow out of this commitment across the days and years that follow. We will keep on speaking of our commitment, keep on saying, "My Lord and my God," with both words and deeds.

What we do will be morally and ethically in tune with the God to whom we have given ourselves. We will work at making past wrongs right. We will become people "for others" just as Christ, our elder brother and high example, was such a person for others. Oh, we'll continue to make mistakes. We will keep on finding blind spots. We certainly will need all the help we can get from the Spirit and from our brothers. But in general our act of confessing that God is our Lord and God will not be a momentary thing but will call forth a new set of relationships that will govern our whole style of living.

SETTING PRIORITIES

Giving ourselves to this God we have named as *our* Lord and *our* God starts speaking right away to how we order our lives. It speaks to what values we place on things and what priorities we give to all that is around us. We can give only so much time, so much energy. We have to choose sometimes between two goods, between better and best.

Many of the priorities we set are going to be determined by what we believe about God and the way he works in the world. If we believe that he is concerned only about how people worship him when they are gathered in the church building, if we believe that he is very particular about just how we do come to him, then we are going to put a form of worship and our particular notion of ortho- dox belief in him above service in his name, above political action in the spirit of Christ, above day-by-day ethical practice in his spirit.

If I believe that God doesn't care much about the fel- lowship of Christians but only our personal relationship, then I am not going to give as high a place to the church and sharing in its life as otherwise. If I believe that he cares primarily about Christians who fully give themselves to him and not much about other people, I am going to pick up that pattern in my own life, too. So all such God- related concepts are going to suggest much about the style of life, the priorities I set for my own actions and concerns as a Christian.

Perhaps you will want to work out for yourself some central affirmations about God that are important to you. Then you can say to yourself, "If this is true, then I am going to live and act this way day by day in my relation with other people: _____."
With that you fill in your own priorities.

So, we have been talking about what might happen when we "bump into God." What happens casually to every man is not likely to remain that way for the person who realizes what is happening and takes the meeting seriously. It becomes for a person a long-term engagement involving God and the person's whole self. He at last comes to the place where he makes some major, deliberate, active response to the God he meets. If with all his mind, strength, body, and spirit, he responds to God's loving redemption and says, "My Lord and my God," he is making a commitment that turns his life around and sets him on a joyous new path.

THINKING THINGS THROUGH

Some Goals

To understand what goes into making a confession and commitment when we acknowledge God as our Lord.

To explore implications for daily living in the making of a commitment of life and self to God.

To examine what all in the self goes into making a commitment to God, what we have to give, what we have to receive in this continuing act.

Some Questions to Consider

1. What all might a person mean when he, like Thomas, says to God (or to something else), "You are my Lord"? What all did Peter mean in response to Jesus' question, "But who do you say that I am?" when he replied, "You are the Christ"?

2. In your own observation what are the most usual things or persons around today that people make into their gods?

3. What do you feel are mistaken or twisted notions about God that people magnify into something central to which they commit themselves when they worship their own notion of God?

4. What are the major priorities for you in commiting your life course to God?

5. How do you know God wants you to make a personal commitment of your life to him?

Some Things to Do

1. Make a list of affirmations about God. Then say, If this is true, then I am going to have to do or be the following:

Then spell out the implications for your life.

2. Describe to another person what it means to make a commitment to God. What all goes into it? How do you proceed? What are the practical results?

3. Write out a list of priorities for your own Christian living and service. What things come first? Discuss with others why you have chosen as you have.